# Working Titles

# Working Titles

# Memoir of an American Hustler

## by Peter Belz

Published by J&S Press, Lancaster, PA

First Edition: 2025

ISBN: 979-8-9930895-0-8

Printed in the United States of America

## Contents

# Working Titles: Memoir of an American Hustler

## By Peter Belz


## Prologue


Baltimore, late '70s.

I was a freshman in high school, not yet a rock star, nor a
rebel, just a kid pushing a mower across rowhouse yards
for a couple of bucks. The smell of cut grass and gasoline
clung to my jeans long after the blades cooled. That was
my first job. Not glamorous, not transformative. Just
sweat, noise, and a little cash in my pocket.

The adults around me kept talking about the future like it
was something you could map out on graph paper.
Guidance counselors, teachers, neighbors --- they all
asked the same question: What are you going to do with
your life? Like there was one clean answer. One career.
One path.

But I didn't have one answer. I had a hundred. Maybe a
thousand. Or maybe none at all.

What followed was sixty-six plus jobs, spread across six
decades. Restaurants, warehouses, trucks, bars, factories.
Some lasted years, some only days. I quit, got fired, got
rehired, got broken down, got back up. I worked with
knives, hoses, pallets, neon's, booze, grease, ink, and
gasoline. I wore aprons, ties, steel-toe boots, name tags,

and tuxedo jackets. I've been the boss, the grunt, the owner, the hired hand.

What I built isn't a résumé. It's a demolition site. Scrap lumber stacked into scaffolding that kept collapsing and being rebuilt into something barely tall enough to get me to the next shift.

This book isn't a celebration. It's not inspiration. It's a record. Of work, of hustles, of all the strange ways a life can be held together when one job isn't enough and one path doesn't exist.

I started cutting grass. I ended up driving fuel tankers. In between, I sold sausages, poured beer, ran restaurants, and scraped grape jelly off trailer floors. Every job left a mark. Some scars, some stories, some regrets.

This is what it looks like when you don't follow the map.

## Introduction

When I was a senior in high school, the administration brought in a career guidance counselor to talk about our futures. I liked those assemblies, not because I cared what the guy had to say, but because it meant I got to dodge a class or two where I hadn't done the homework. Free period dressed up as life advice.

One thing he said stuck. He told us that my father's generation could expect one job their whole life, maybe two, in rare cases three. But times had changed, he warned. Because of shifting economics, my generation could expect as many as five or six jobs or careers. He stressed the importance of planning, mapping out our futures right then and there.

At eighteen, the only future planning I cared about was figuring out where the parties were that weekend and if there'd be beer left by the time I got there. That was about as far down the road as I could see.

What I didn't know at the time was just how wrong the man was, and how right. He was correct that the world of work was changing, but five or six jobs? I burned through that number before most people finished freshman year of college. What followed wasn't a neat résumé with promotions climbing politely toward retirement. It was a mess: hustles, stints, gigs, and small-time disasters stacked like splintered lumber after a demolition.

At a certain point, I realized I was becoming a jack of all trades. And I started to wear it like a badge. The line everyone loved to toss out, jack of all trades, master of none, was always meant as an insult. What they didn't know was that the full saying is: jack of all trades, master of none, but always better than a master of one. That's not a dig. That's a salute. A recognition that versatility is its own kind of mastery, especially in a world that never stops shifting under your feet.

I wasn't climbing a single ladder. I was patching together bridges from scraps, stringing wires between collapsing buildings, building boats out of driftwood to cross rivers I didn't even know were there until I was already knee-deep in them. The bet wasn't on stability. It was on survival, and sometimes on chaos, just to keep life interesting.

I've worked more jobs than I can count, and every single one left a mark. Sometimes it was a scar. Sometimes just a story you tell later in a bar over beer and a whiskey. Sometimes just enough cash to cover rent and a greasy takeout meal. With each paycheck came another lesson: how to sharpen a knife without slicing your thumb off, how to bounce a drunk without catching a right hook, how to fake confidence in front of a boss who knows you're bluffing but lets it slide anyway. Taken together, the collection doesn't make me a specialist. It makes me a generalist in the oldest school there is---the school of survival.

The dates and timelines in these pages won't always line up neatly. Memory blurs, records were never neat, and half the time I was too busy or too stoned or too beat down to care. But the spirit is true. What matters isn't the calendar---it's the grind, the faces, the odd little lessons I dragged home from every gig.

From mowing lawns behind Baltimore row houses, to sweating under banquet lights pouring wine in tuxedo tails, to running my own café in a town most people couldn't place on a map, to screaming punk songs in clubs where the ceiling tiles rained dust, this is the story of a lifetime of work. Sometimes it was survival, sometimes adventure, sometimes pure stupidity. But it was always motion. Always hustle.

I didn't climb a career ladder. I built a scaffold, fell off it, dragged the lumber with me, then hammered it into something else. This isn't career advice. It's a witness statement.

If there's wisdom here, it wasn't earned in classrooms. It was bought shift by shift, scar by scar, hour by hour. Consider this the receipt.

## Job #1 – Lawn Mower – Age 12 – 1976

And the first line on that receipt? Me, twelve years old, moist from a humid Baltimore summer, pushing a lawn mower that looked like a medieval torture device. The cracked row house sidewalks rattled the wheels, sweat stung my eyes, and every spin of the blades sounded like an angry cicada on meth. Childhood chores had a way of mutating into side hustles, and before long, I was in business --- whether I meant to be or not.

This wasn't some gas-powered beast that roared through the block, ripping lawns down to velvet in minutes. No --- this was the old-school reel mower, the kind with the whirring, spinning blades that only cut if you ran it like hell. Slow down, and the blades just folded the grass over like a bad comb-over on a drunk uncle. Every pass was cardio, every yard a marathon. By the time I finished, my legs were jelly, my arms screamed, and I smelled like a sweaty rag dipped in cat piss.

Once the grass was down, I moved on to the manual edger --- a medieval contraption with iron teeth that chewed through grass and dirt alike, if you shoved it hard enough. The sidewalks balked, my palms blistered, and the line I carved looked more like trench warfare than landscaping. It wasn't pretty, but it got the job done.

The first time I ever knocked on a stranger's door to pitch my services, I was shaking. Voice cracking, palms wet, brain screaming don't screw this up. I hadn't even figured out what "lawn mowing" meant yet --- front yard only? Back too? Did edging count? Sweeping? Pulling weeds? It was all a blur. And then I made the dumbest rookie mistake imaginable: I told the guy he could pay me whatever he thought it was worth.

Big mistake.

I mowed front and back, edged the walk, swept the place clean like the Mayor's parade was coming through. Hours later, dripping and streaked with perspiration, I knocked back on his door. He smiled, handed me a single dollar, and said, "Great job." That dollar burned hotter than the sun. Lesson learned: never let the customer set your price. From then on, my minimum was three bucks.

Family was better business. My grandparents paid me five dollars a lawn, and in 1976, five bucks was a fortune. Kiss, Aerosmith, Sabbath --- $4.99 plus tax. A Saturday morning sweating in their backyard meant walking home with an album tucked under my arm, still fresh from the record store bin. But their generosity came with strings. My grandmother was the toughest foreman I ever had. Arms crossed, eagle-eyed, she'd call out every missed strip, every rogue blade of grass. "Back it up. You missed a spot. Sweep again. Don't leave clippings in the flower bed." I earned those fives the hard way, strip by strip, lecture by lecture.

By age fourteen, my dad upgraded me to a gas mower, and suddenly the game changed. What once ate an entire afternoon now took half the time. I felt like I'd harnessed the power of modern civilization. A year later he brought home a gas-powered weed wacker, and that's when I reached my artistic peak. I was the Michelangelo of lawncare --- carving sharp edges and clean lines with the same precision the Renaissance masters brought to marble.

By the end of that summer, I had a full-fledged hustle. Nervous knocks on stranger's doors, cheap neighbors who thought I was only worth a buck, grandparents doubling as quality-control inspectors, and long afternoons running that cicada-blade mower until my arms gave out. It was my first business, my first real hustle.

And the lesson stayed with me: always set your own price, never undersell the effort, and for Pete's sake, don't leave clippings on the walk.

## Job #2: Snow Shoveler – Age 12 – 1976

Snow shoveling wasn't like mowing lawns. Lawns waited for you, grass grew slow, patient. Snow was a hit-and-run job. You had to strike while it was fresh, before it turned into ankle-deep concrete under a hundred footprints and car tires. It was timing, hustle, and a little bit of territorial warfare.

In Baltimore row house neighborhoods, opportunity was everywhere. Every house had a sidewalk, and every sidewalk was a potential paycheck. But back then nobody had a snow blower. Those belonged to suburban dreamers in cul-de-sac kingdoms. In the city, it was just kids like me with a bent shovel, a stiff broom, and enough caffeine-free sugar in our veins from Kool-Aid and Pop-Tarts to get through a storm.

The trick was to get out early, when the snow was still powder, when you could carve a clean line down a block before the guy two streets over caught on and hustled in on your territory. I'd knock doors, pitch my services, and then dive in like some polar explorer, hacking paths through the drifts.

Four or five bucks a sidewalk was the going rate. Fair enough for forty-five minutes of sweat and frozen fingers. I'd shovel it clean, then always finish with the broom, sweeping until the walk looked crisp, polished, like a stage waiting for the star to make their entrance.

And when it snowed steady, it felt like a hustle. Fast money, crisp bills in my pocket, a hot chocolate waiting somewhere down the line.

But then came the big ones. The blizzards of '78 and '82. The kind of storms that turned Baltimore into a whiteout prison camp. Ten-foot drifts, cars swallowed whole, entire blocks erased under a sheet of frozen white.

For a teenager with a shovel, it should've been paradise, a gold rush of sidewalks. But there was a fatal flaw in my business model: I was charging by the job, not the hour.

Four bucks for forty-five minutes? Fine. Four bucks for three hours of backbreaking, boot-soaking, bone-shivering labor? That was masochism. Each load of snow heavier than the last, my arms screaming, my back shot, and the math getting worse every second.

At some point I dropped the shovel, looked at the mountain in front of me, and realized I'd rather be a kid than a martyr. The best sledding of my life happened during those storms. We built ramps out of plowed drifts, launched ourselves like human missiles, and came home with faces red from windburn and hearts pounding from the thrill of flight.

That winter, I learned two things. One: never let your pricing bury you alive. Two: sometimes the better payday is a hill, a sled, and the kind of joy that makes you forget you're broke.

**Job #3: Paper Boy – Age 12 – 1976**

If lawn mowing was steady work and snow shoveling was a hustle, being a paper boy was my first taste of logistics. Not the clean, bar-coded Amazon Prime kind, but the raw, analog grind of a twelve-year-old hauling dead trees and ink around Baltimore. It was me against gravity, me against time, and me against a sack of newspapers that weighed as much as I did.

I delivered the evening and Sunday editions of **The Baltimore Sun**. Weekdays meant hoofing it after school, lugging a canvas sack over my shoulder until the straps dug trenches in my skin. Sundays were a different animal. The paper was so bloated with ads and inserts it had to be split into two deliveries. Saturday brought the "lite" version, coupons and comics and recipes and what not, and then Sunday was the real monster, a brick of newsprint so heavy it could throw out your back before puberty even hit.

My route wasn't in Hampden, the working-class row house neighborhood where I lived. Nope, the Sun decided to export me north into Roland Park, where Baltimore's money slept behind manicured hedges and polished doors. Delivering there was like sneaking into another dimension. Their sidewalks were longer, their porches were bigger, and their expectations were sharper. You didn't just toss the paper on their lawn and run. It had to land neat, dry, and close to the door. These people didn't want news, they wanted service.

I had a secret weapon: my skateboard. Most paper boys trudged along, dragging their sacks like condemned men. I bombed those quiet Roland Park streets on four urethane wheels, bag swinging, firing newspapers at porches like some wild-eyed twelve-year-old courier of doom. The skateboard cut my route time in half, but it also meant I lived on the edge of catastrophe. Baltimore sidewalks are war zones. Cracks, tree roots, uneven seams --- each one a landmine that could stop the board dead and send me flying, papers scattering like confetti at a parade.

There was one hill in particular, a long, steep plunge that made or broke the route. At the top, the choice was yours: bail and walk it like a coward, or drop in and trust your legs not to shake apart. I usually chose the latter. Controlling the board with a hundred pounds of newspaper strapped to me was lunacy. The trick was to keep just enough speed to stay balanced, but not so much that you overshot the porch or rocketed into the intersection like a human missile. When I stuck the landing --- paper thudding perfectly against the door --- it felt like Olympic gold. When I missed, I perfected the art of the sheepish apology.

Collecting money was its own side hustle. Some Roland Park families tipped like I was delivering lost treasure, folding crisp bills into my hand with a smile, "keep the change". Others treated me like I was running a scam, digging through couch cushions to scrape together exact change, their suspicion hanging in the air like stale cigar smoke.

And then came the jackpot. One afternoon, a customer opened the door, a guy in his thirties, and casually asked if I liked comic books. "Yes!" I blurted out, my twelve-year-old brain already racing. He told me he had a couple of boxes he didn't want anymore. Free. I nearly levitated. The only problem was logistics again --- I was on my skateboard. No way to haul boxes. So the next day I returned with my dad, and we loaded them into the car.

It was a gold mine. Spiderman, Hulk, Thor, Iron Man, Batman, The Archies, G.I. Joe, dusty westerns, psychedelic side stories, and dozens I'd never seen before. Hours and hours of stories poured into my lap. It was like the universe had expanded overnight, and my paper route had opened the wormhole.

The job wasn't glamorous. It was hard work and balancing acts, skateboard wheels rattling, newspapers cutting into my shoulder, and that constant gamble with gravity. But it was also freedom. Twelve years old, bombing down Roland Park hills at sunset with the news of the world slung across my chest. And on that one perfect day, it was more than just cash in my pocket. It was the day the paper route didn't just deliver the Sun --- it delivered me into what would become the multiverse.

### Job #4: Janitor – Age 16 – 1980

I landed the janitor job at the **HR Clinic** in Hampden thanks to my cousin Rose, who worked there and slid me in through the back door. The place was a repurposed church, tucked next to the library, and it still carried the drafty bones of its past life. Stained glass windows stared down at peeling paint. Instead of hymns and sermons, it now offered the neighborhood free medical checkups, childcare, donated food, and whatever else could be patched together on a shoestring.

It wasn't glamorous work. Hell, it wasn't even work you wanted to talk about. My shift started after the doors locked for the night, and my role was simple: clean up the wreckage left behind by a day's worth of struggling humanity. Empty trash cans stuffed with paper cups, mop scuffed floors tracked with mud, sweep up crumbs from the kids' snack rooms. Easy enough, until I hit the back rooms.

That was where things got real. Exam tables with soiled paper still crumpled across them. Gauze, medical tape and fluids nobody ever taught me the names for. By today's standards, half of it would've required a hazmat suit, full face shield, and a biohazard bag. Back then, I had a mop and bucket, and the optimism of being sixteen. When you're standing alone in a repurposed church at midnight mopping up who-knows-what, optimism is all you've got.

I wasn't paid by the hour. Flat rate, no overtime, no dragging my feet to make it last. Whether it took me three hours or forty minutes, the check was the same. So I went fast. The less time I spent hovering over what looked suspiciously like a crime scene, the better.

But the job came with one perk that outweighed the filth: they gave me a key. That was a dangerous thing to hand a sixteen-year-old kid who'd just started to party. On more than one weekend, I'd tell my parents I was crashing at a friend's place, then go to a party and drink until the ground tilted. Instead of stumbling home, I'd slip into the clinic, lock the door, and stretch out on an exam table like it was my personal crash pad. The same tables I cleaned up after others on, I now passed out on myself.

By Saturday at 5 p.m., when the doors locked, the place was mine. My own private hideout, lit by fluorescent hum and the smell of antiseptic. On paper, I was the janitor. In reality, I was a kid with keys to an empty building, equal parts custodian, squatter, and minor outlaw.

The clinic gave me a paycheck, but more than that, it gave me a secret clubhouse where the rent was sweat and bleach. If I had to mop up something unspeakable now and then to keep the privilege, well, that was the price of admission.

### Job #5: Switchboard Operator – Age 17 – 1981

By the time I was a junior in high school, my weekends were split between the homework I didn't want to do and the jobs I actually did. One of the stranger gigs was working the switchboard at the **Highfield House**, a modernist high-rise in Baltimore that still looked sharp, all clean lines and quiet luxury. It was the kind of place with polished lobbies, uniformed doormen in white gloves, who would valet the Cadillacs and Mercedes into the garage.

Meanwhile, I was tucked behind a desk at the switchboard, headset on, the polite gatekeeper for Baltimore's well-heeled. Every call passed through me first. "Good evening, Highfield House, who may I say is calling?" If the resident upstairs wanted to take it, I connected them. If not, I scribbled a message on a slip and slid it into their mailbox. On paper, I was just a messenger. In practice, I was a teenage kid running comms for people who lived in a different world.

The manager's office sat just beyond the board, complete with its own waiting room. Since the manager never came in on weekends, it became my clubhouse. Friends would swing by with a six-pack or a joint, and we'd laugh too loud behind the closed door while the residents upstairs sipped martinis and hosted cocktail parties. To them, I was invisible, a polite voice on the phone. In the back room, I was running my own private lounge.

Not every surprise was fun. One afternoon, I opened the staff bathroom door and found Maurice, one of the doormen, sitting on the toilet lid, tying off and shooting heroin. He didn't flinch, didn't even look up. Just pressed the plunger like I wasn't there. I muttered, "Maybe you should lock the door," and went back to my post. My first up-close encounter with hard drugs wasn't in a back alley---it was twenty feet from the marble lobby, inside one of Baltimore's nicest addresses.

And then there was the resident who came down for his messages. Late twenties, flamboyant, sharply dressed. As he leaned in, I caught a whiff of weed. Without hesitation, I asked if he had an extra joint. He looked shocked for half a second, then smirked and handed one over. I still can't believe I had the nerve. At seventeen, it never occurred to me that I could get fired for that. Consequences were abstract. Missing out wasn't.

That was the job in a nutshell: a study in contrasts. Out front, marble floors, white gloves, and quiet wealth.

Behind the board, teenagers sneaking beers, a doorman nodding off on heroin, and a resident slipping me weed.

Highfield House wasn't just a job. It was my first glimpse of how the shiny world of money and respectability always has a back room---and sometimes the real stories are hiding there, not in the lobby.

### Job #6: Office Mover – Age 17 – 1981

A high school buddy's mom worked for a company called **E.I. Kane Office Movers,** and every so often they needed extra bodies. We weren't hauling sofas out of row houses or pianos up brownstone staircases. These guys moved entire businesses. Whole floors of skyscrapers stripped down to the studs overnight. Desks, chairs, filing cabinets, typewriters, metal wastebaskets, even the framed motivational posters that no one had looked at in years. Corporate life, boxed and tagged, ready to vanish from one high rise and reappear in another by sunrise.

The hours were brutal: 11 p.m. to 7 a.m. We clocked in when the city was winding down, and by the time the rest of Baltimore was groggily pouring its first cup of coffee, we'd been breaking our backs for eight hours, hauling furniture through labyrinths of beige hallways, cramming it into freight elevators that smelled like decades of dust and sweat, and shoving it onto trucks waiting like open mouths at the loading docks. At the other end, we reassembled the mess so that, come Monday morning, the bosses could sit down at their desks as if nothing had happened. Like magic. Except the trick was powered by cheap labor and strong backs.

My friend Bill got me and a couple of other prep school softies in the door. We were the aliens on the crew, boys with clean hands and nervous smiles dropped into a world of hard men with prison-yard tans, knuckles like scar tissue, tattoos that looked like they'd been carved with a penknife in a cellblock. These guys had faces like road maps of every bad decision they'd ever made. We stuck out immediately, the contrast almost cartoonish.

But we learned fast. From them we picked up the art of vanishing, which was just as important as the art of lifting. You found an empty closet, locked conference room, or forgotten supply nook, shut the door, sparked up whatever you had, and disappeared for an hour. It was hide-and-seek with paychecks. As long as you emerged dripping sweat and looking miserable, no one asked questions. We got paid to move offices, but the real lesson was how to make time disappear.

The pros also taught us another kind of hustle. I wasn't tempted, but it was impossible not to notice. Lamps, trash bins, paper cutters, the occasional desk fan—small, easy-to-miss stuff had a way of "vanishing" in the shuffle. You could see the practiced way a guy would clock something, shift it slightly, and make sure it was staged near the truck door for an easy exit. They weren't just moving offices; they were running their own five-finger clearance sale on the side.

The work itself was monotonous, but the scale was mesmerizing. Watching an entire company uprooted and transplanted overnight was surreal. Offices that had been buzzing with phones and typewriters one afternoon were stripped bare by morning, like a crime scene after the evidence had been hauled away. To me, it was just another paycheck, another night of aching arms and sore feet, but the bigger picture stuck with me. Whole lives, whole businesses could be dismantled, packed, and shipped like they never existed.

By the end of a shift, my shirt was soaked through, my hands blistered, and my head buzzing from the combination of fatigue, weed, and fluorescent lighting. It wasn't a job I loved, or even liked, but it was one more notch on the stick. One more strange chapter in the long book of hustles.

Office moving didn't teach me how to build a career, but it did show me two things: that most work is just organized chaos, and that even the most boring gig has a shadow economy humming beneath the surface.

### Job #7: Fish Monger – Age 17+ – 1981

Another weekend job I picked up while I was still in high school, but one that carried over into full-time work after I graduated, was at **Faidley's Seafood** in Baltimore's Lexington Market. For context, Lexington Market isn't just another shopping spot, it's the oldest public market in the United States. The place is a legend, and on Saturdays it felt like half the city had crammed inside its walls.

Faidley's was a madhouse of ice, fish, and shouting vendors. Customers pressed up to the counter, pointing at fillets or whole fish while we hustled to keep up. As a fish monger, my job was sales --- take the orders, scoop, weigh, wrap, and bark the battle cry of the stall. Bill, the owner, was a retired military man with a fat cigar permanently clamped in his teeth, not smoked, just chewed into pulp. He had us constantly hollering "Help ya! May we help!" at anyone who wandered within earshot. It was part sales pitch, part drill sergeant bark, and it kept the stall moving like a machine.

I got a couple of my buddies, Matt and Mike, jobs there too. Working side by side with them made the chaos fun. Lexington Market was a wild place, a revolving cast of characters wandered its aisles, from old-timers to hustlers to families doing their shopping. On occasion, even Divine would show up at Faidley's raw bar. It was a standing bar, no stools, no chairs, just counters where people crowded in to slurp oysters and pick crabs. Divine would hold court in the middle of it all, dressed in some outrageous outfit --- once a pink terrycloth robe and slippers --- and stop the market cold. Heads turned, whispers spread, and even in that madhouse of fishmongers and shouting vendors, Divine stole the spotlight.

We mongers weren't the cutters --- that was a separate crew of full-time guys with blades moving so fast they could make a salmon look like lace in under a minute. But when things slowed down, they let me hang close and pick up tricks. I practiced until I could gut, scale, and fillet a fish with some competence. Not their level, but enough to give me confidence and a skill set that would come in handy later in kitchens.

And it wasn't just fish. We sold things I never imagined people ate --- turtles, muskrats, even bags of fish heads. The old-timers swore the best meat was in the head. Crabmeat wasn't the luxury item it is today, either. Back then I'd buy a pound of backfin for a few bucks and eat it straight out of the container on the bus ride home.

Downstairs was another world entirely. Beneath the market sat a dungeon-like basement where businesses kept their storage. Concrete cells, no roofs, just walls you could hop if you knew the right spot. The lighting was dim, the air damp, and the floor alive with the scurrying of rats. A couple of picnic tables sat in the middle, meant for employees to eat lunch in peace.

Naturally, we turned it into our hideout. We'd hop a wall into the storage room, light up, and smoke weed until the air was foggy enough to slice with a fillet knife. Afterward we'd sprawl at the picnic tables, eat our lunches, and watch the rats dart back and forth like they were commuters in some kind of underground subway system. It was gross, it was grimy, and it was ours.

The bus rides home were their own comedy. Picture a group of teenage fishmongers piling onto the back of the bus after a shift, stinking of fish so badly that every head turned. You could actually watch the wave of disgust ripple through the passengers. People sniffing, wrinkling noses, craning their necks to figure out what the hell smelled so bad. It was us, and there was nothing we could do about it. We just sat there, reeking and smiling.

Working at Faidley's wasn't glamorous, but it gave me two things: a paycheck, and knife skills I picked up on the side, skills sharp enough to carve out future jobs in kitchens. It also taught me something else --- that behind every historic landmark and "authentic" market experience, there's a basement full of rats, a couple of teenagers getting high, and a raw bar where Divine might show up in slippers and a robe to steal the show.

**Job #8: Deck Hand – Age 18 – 1982**

After slinging fish at Faidley's, my next hustle took me off land and onto water, with **Baltimore Patriot Tours** at the newly christened Baltimore Inner Harbor. The company ran two double-decker boats, crammed with tourists, out past Fort McHenry, down to the Key Bridge, and back again --- a three-hour tour straight out of Gilligan's Island, minus the coconut radios and slapstick shipwreck.

At first, my job was grunt-level simple. Get the passengers on board, untie the ropes, and once we were moving, hustle hot dogs, candy bars, and sodas from the snack stand while trying not to faceplant every time the boat rocked. The crowds were a mix: locals who wanted to show off Baltimore's shiny new waterfront, and out-of-towners hoping for a bite-sized version of "authentic Baltimore."

The real payoff came later, when they let me grab the mic and run the tour. That's when it stopped being a job and became a stage. The script had the usual dry historical points, but I couldn't resist putting some of myself into it. There was the Maryland National (MN) building, looming over the harbor with its big colored lights coded for incoming ships. The official line went like this:

"When it's red, warm weather ahead.

When it's blue, cool weather for you.

When it's yellow, the weather's quite mellow."

That was the canned spiel. My version tacked on a final punchline:

"When it's pink with purple polka dots... GET THE HELL OUT OF TOWN!"

It killed every time. For an eighteen-year-old barely out of high school, holding a microphone on the deck of a boat, skyline glittering behind me while a boat load of strangers laughed at my jokes, it felt like I'd found a new kind of oxygen.

Perks came with the gig. When the tourists were gone, we had access to a little dinghy. After work or off-duty nights, we'd cruise the Inner Harbor like a pack of teenage monarchs, beers in hand, no plan except motion. One Fourth of July we floated under the fireworks, so close the ash and sparks rained down on us like we were extras in Apocalypse Now. It felt reckless, maybe stupid, but perfect --- Baltimore lit up in fire above us, the dinghy rocking gently below.

And then there was Captain Udo. The man was a character straight out of central casting. A race car crash had cost him a leg, and now he stomped around on a prosthetic, part limp, part swagger. Gruff voice, sharp edges, a lifetime of stories tucked behind his smirk. One night I was loitering on the dock, waiting on a girl I'd been chasing, hoping she'd finally show so we could head to a party together. Udo clomped by, already halfway gone, and stopped just long enough to give me one line that lodged itself in my brain:

"Never wait around for someone else. Life's too short. She'll catch up."

Simple. Brutal. True. Advice from a one-legged captain that landed heavier than any sermon or guidance counselor pep talk ever did.

Baltimore Patriot Tours gave me a paycheck, sure. But it also handed me a microphone, a dinghy under exploding fireworks, and a piece of advice that's stuck with me ever since. Don't wait around. Just go.

### Job #9: Inventory Manager – Age 19 – 1983

Some jobs last years. Some last months. This one lasted exactly one week.

I got hired by **Fiske Catering** as their "inventory manager." It sounded like a title with weight, like I was going to be running logistics for some glamorous culinary operation. The reality? I was lord of a dusty storeroom stacked with folding tables, stacks of plates, bins of silverware, towers of linens, battered chafing dishes, and every piece of rental catering crap you could imagine. My job was to keep it neat, make sure the trucks got loaded with the right gear, and when it all came slouching back covered in grease, ash, and who knows what else, count it, clean it, and get it ready for the next wedding or fundraiser. A glorified quartermaster for rented forks.

Still, I didn't mind it. There was a certain satisfaction in order, in stacking things just so, in making sense out of chaos. I thought maybe, just maybe, I'd stumbled onto something steady. But the universe has always had a way of teaching me that "steady" was not in my vocabulary.

The breaking point came fast. One weekend I headed out to the Maryland Hunt Cup, the kind of horse-racing event where the equestrian prestige is real, but so is the binge drinking. It had poured rain the night before, so by the time I got there the grounds were a mud pit. I was wearing flip-flops, which quickly turned into useless, slimy anchors. I ditched them and went barefoot, figuring it was the smart move.

Bad call. What I didn't know was that the grounds crew had hacked down and burned a mountain of poison ivy to prep the fields. And I, lucky bastard that I am, was highly allergic. By the next morning, my feet looked like special effects makeup --- ballooned, oozing, grotesque. Shoes were impossible. Standing was impossible. Pretty much anything except lying on the floor and cursing the fates was impossible.

I called in to say I needed a couple days to recover. Their response was short and cold: "You're fired." That was it.

A week in, and my catering career was over. Easy come, easier go.

At the time, I was living in a basement apartment near the Maryland Institute College of Art with my buddy Mike, who was actually attending school while I was just free-floating through life. Losing the job wasn't just about a missed paycheck. It was a domino that tipped everything else over --- rent, food, and, most importantly back then, drugs. Priorities weren't complicated. Rent and food were afterthoughts. Drugs were the main course.

The apartment itself was a den of chaos. You never knew who'd come knocking on that basement door off the trash-can-lined alley. Friends, strangers, hangers-on, junkies --- they all cycled through. The bathroom saw things I'll never describe in print. Parties spilled across the floor, nights bled into mornings, and the haze of smoke never quite cleared.

But the roaches --- that's what I remember most. Millions of them. They weren't pests, they were residents. They owned that place. We started keeping spray bottles filled with water so we could sharpshoot them off the walls. It turned into a game --- who could drop one in a single squirt. It was disgusting, sure, but when you're nineteen, high, and broke, disgusting becomes normal.

Eventually, I couldn't pay my share of the rent. Mike stayed, and I drifted. Losing the job wasn't just about losing steady work --- it was a collapse, a slip deeper into the chaos I was racing headlong into. One week of organizing forks and linens, one barefoot night of bad luck, and suddenly I was jobless, apartmentless, and watching the scaffolding of my life sag under its own weight.

## Job #10: Dishwasher, Prep Cook, Line Cook – Age 19 – 1983

The **Museum Café** was my first real restaurant job, though I didn't exactly land it in any glamorous way. My buddy Greg was bussing there and said, "Hey, we need a dishwasher. You want it?" I was broke, unemployed, and looking for something --- anything --- so I said yes on the spot.

Dishwashing was exactly what you'd expect, and somehow worse. Endless racks of plates, each one crusted with food that had solidified into something closer to concrete than cuisine. Steam poured off the machine until the back room felt like a sauna nobody in their right mind would pay for. The floor was always slick, the pans never stopped coming, and no matter how fast I worked, there was always another mountain waiting. My hands reeked of bleach, my clothes of fryer grease. The dish pit was hell with fluorescent lighting.

I stuck it out for three or so months. Bleach burns on my hands, grease embedded in my pores, coming home every night with the smell of the kitchen clinging like a curse. It was bottom rung pay, barely bus fare money, but it was something.

Then one day, everything changed. The sous chef didn't show --- again --- off on one of his epic benders. The chef was pacing like a madman because a delivery of rainbow trout had just landed, and they had to be filleted for that night's special. Normally that was the sous chef's job, but the guy was MIA and panic was rising.

I spoke up. "I'll fillet them."

The chef stopped dead, looked me over --- nineteen years old, bleach-stained apron, sweat-soaked, with my crazy new wave hair sticking out in every direction --- and burst out laughing. "You? Fillet these? HA! HA! HA!" The whole kitchen joined in.

I told him I used to work in a fish market. He rolled his eyes, shoved a flat at me, and gave me the threat: butcher one fish, and I'd spend the day scrubbing garbage cans.

I grabbed the knife, laid the trout on the board, and went to work. Clean, precise, fast. By the time I finished the first fillet, the laughter had died. By the time I finished the whole flat, the chef's jaw had dropped. He handed me another flat. Then another. When both were done, perfect and ready for service, he gave me a single nod. That was it. I was no longer the dishwasher. I was running the cold side and doing prep.

One of the other prep cooks I met there, Peter, like me, needed an apartment so we got a place together. Things were looking up as we created a cool, third story apartment in Charles Village. Including a dark room for black and white photography, which we took advantage of often.

I hustled my way onto the hot line. I went from scraping pans, to cold side, to hot side --- a line cook firing plates out to paying customers. The catch? The pay didn't change. I was still on dishwasher wages, too naïve to push back.

When the original chef split, the new one came in. Instead of easing into the existing system, he relied on me --- a nineteen-year-old --- to show him how things ran. I was training the chef who was supposed to be training me, all while still making dish pit money.

But here's the thing about restaurant work: even when it screws you, it becomes a family. The crew was my tribe. After service, we'd hit the bars, throw wild parties, rent sailboats, sprawl in city parks, chasing life together. The chaos of the kitchen, the burns, the smoke breaks --- all of it bonded us tighter than the paycheck ever could.

Years later, thanks to social media, I still see their faces. Older, sure, but familiar. And every time one pops up, it's like a phantom smell of steam, bleach, and fryer oil drifting back. A ghost of the dish pit.

Eventually, I'd had enough. After carrying the place, training chefs, and pulling more weight than anyone else at my level, I finally asked for a raise. The chef promised me a whole dollar an hour --- massive at the time. When the paycheck came, I checked the numbers: twenty-five cents. A slap in the face dressed up as generosity.

I was furious. I didn't show up that Friday night. Didn't show up the next day either. When I finally came back, it was only to grab my last check. The chef lost it, screaming that I'd abandoned the line, left him stranded. I told him to go fuck himself, for stiffing me on the raise.

It's the only job I've ever walked out on. And it branded me with one of the most important lessons I've carried since: never let anyone else tell you what you're worth. Because if you do, you'll spend your life stuck in the dish pit, sweating for pennies, while someone else cashes in on your knife skills.


**Job #11: Waiter – Age 21 – 1985**


I only landed the job because I was dating the floor manager. She slid me into a waiter position even though I had zero experience. I didn't hesitate. I'd been watching the servers strut out with cash-heavy pockets while the cooks slogged through the grease and heat for scraps. Less sweat, more money, better hours. Easy choice.

It was a trial by fire. My very first shift was a lunch service at the **Owl Bar** in the Belvedere Hotel. Lunch at the Owl was not training-wheels territory. The place was crawling with lawyers, bankers, and business types, all of them with thirty minutes to eat and the self-importance of Roman emperors. You could read the hierarchy on sight: the bosses leaned back with martinis, unbothered by the clock, while the underlings ordered iced tea and asked for the check before their sandwiches even hit the table. My job was to sprint in their shadow, scribbling orders, dodging elbows, and laying down plates fast enough to keep them from reminding me that their time was worth more than my life.

The Owl Bar had its share of characters, but none burned into my memory like The Colonel. Tall, thin, always immaculate in his white suit, vest, and matching hat, he looked like he'd stepped out of an old British war film. He spoke in a clipped accent, the kind that made every sentence sound like an order, and carried himself like a man who once commanded battalions and wasn't about to stop now.

But The Colonel wasn't there for the food. His devotion was reserved for crème de menthe. Green, sticky, liquid candy. He'd sit in the alcove entrance and work his way through glass after glass, until the mint liquor dripped down the deep creases in his weathered face and stained his white trousers emerald. By late afternoon he'd be slurring loudly enough to rattle the windows, and someone would have to haul him across the hotel lobby and stuff him into a cab. Most servers refused to touch his table. I was the only one who did.

One afternoon he asked for my full name. He wrote it carefully in a notebook. The next time he arrived, he handed me several pages of paper. At the top, in neat script, was the title: "Lines to Peter Paul Belz III."

He had written me a poem. Lines about loyalty, companionship, carrying him through the rough patches. It was strange, moving, and more intimate than I was prepared for. He read some of it aloud to me, voice wavering between soldierly command and drunken slur.

Then, before he left, he asked for the poem back. I didn't keep a copy. I wish I had.

Later I learned The Colonel wasn't just some eccentric drunk in a white suit. He was a decorated British veteran of World War I, a published poet who had written about his war years. I still wonder if somewhere, buried in a forgotten book, there's a poem about me --- a young waiter in Baltimore --- remembered by a fading soldier drowning in crème de menthe.

Not every customer came wrapped in mystery and pathos. One afternoon I served a couple who ate like royalty: cocktails, appetizers, entrées, desserts, the full ride. When the bill came, the man flagged me down. He apologized. They didn't have enough cash for a tip, and he didn't want to put it on his credit card --- people were skittish about that back then. "I'll get you next time," he said, handing me his business card. He owned Luskin's, the local furniture store chain. Their slogan? "The cheapest guy in town." He wasn't kidding.

And then there was the day Tears for Fears blew through. They were staying at the Belvedere while on tour. They rolled into the Owl Bar with their entourage, ordered drinks, and I figured why not shoot my shot. After dropping a round at their table, I asked if they could spare a couple passes to the show. One of them didn't even blink --- just snapped, "Piss off!" Welcome to rock and roll.

The Owl Bar was a crash course in human theater. Martini-swilling bosses, iced-tea clerks, eccentric war heroes, bargain-basement moguls, and pop stars telling me to fuck off. Every table had its own play, its own absurd lesson. For me, it wasn't just waiting tables. It was a study in character, a front-row seat to Baltimore's mix of grit and grandeur, and a reminder that every job, no matter how temporary, leaves a story worth keeping.

## Job #12: Fine Dining Waiter – Age 22 – 1986

The **John Eager Howard Room** was nothing like the Owl Bar. Also tucked inside the Belvedere Hotel, it was a formal dining restaurant where men were required to wear jackets, and the walls were covered in vast murals painted in the 1930s. The place dripped with old-world formality.

The maître d', James, approached me one day after seeing me at the Owl Bar. He told me he liked my look, had heard I was a good server, and asked me to come work for him. The Howard Room was another world entirely: tuxedos with tails, white gloves, full French Service. Every detail mattered. I cleaned up well, sharp and polished, because in a room like that, appearance wasn't optional.

Two hours before opening, we'd begin the ritual: setting up our sections, arranging silverware and glassware in perfect alignment, steam-polishing everything until it gleamed, stacking and resetting until the tables looked like museum displays. It was a performance before the performance.

On my first day flying solo, a well-dressed couple sat in my section and ordered an $80 bottle of wine right away, an astronomical sum in 1986. I brought the bottle to the table, cut the foil, slid the corkscrew in, and eased it out. The cork gave the faintest little pop.

The man's head snapped toward me. "What did you do?! You just ruined that bottle of wine! Get away from this table and take that wine with you! You're an abomination of a waiter; I don't want to see you again!"

I slunk away, crushed, hiding behind the bus station. James had seen the whole thing. He reassigned the table and came over to me: "Don't worry. That guy was just being a prick." After the shift, we shared that "ruined" bottle. It was delicious.

We entered the Howard Room through a service entrance at the back of the hotel and up a flight of stairs to the kitchen. There was also a VIP elevator, a sleek, private lift running from the basement to the Penthouse suite, with a door that opened right at the entrance to the dining room. Staff weren't allowed to use it. One day, late for work, I broke the rule and took the VIP elevator to save time.

The doors swung open, and I stepped out, straight into several men in black suits. They grabbed me hard, jostled me about and demanded who I was and what I was doing. As it turned out, Archbishop Desmond Tutu was dining at the John Eager Howard Room that day, and the place was on lockdown for his protection. Once I convinced them I was just a server and not some threat, they let me go. I caught heat from management for it, but mostly it was a lesson in how badly "shortcut thinking" can backfire.

But the biggest change in my life at the Howard Room didn't come from wine snobs or security run-ins. It came from a coworker. That's where I met Yuri, a Russian immigrant server who was also an incredible artist. After work one night, he invited me back to his apartment. I brought hash, thinking we'd smoke. While I was breaking it up, I noticed Yuri tying off his arm and fixing up a needle.

I'd seen heroin before, but this was different. "I thought you wanted to smoke up?" I asked. He shrugged. "That shit does nothing for me." Then he plunged the needle and asked if I wanted to try. That night I said no. The next day, I said yes.

In short time, I had gotten so good at fixing myself that I could sneak down to a barely used basement bathroom in the hotel and take care of business in about five minutes flat. What had started as hesitation turned into habit, and habit into a routine that fit neatly between courses of French Service.

Here my story takes a darker turn. I went back and forth on whether to include this part at all. I'm not proud of it. But it was a big part of my life then, and it rippled into my future jobs and choices. The Howard Room was where I slid from weekend warrior into everyday addict. It was a job of tuxedos, white gloves, French service, and Depression-era murals towering over the room, but beneath all that formality, I was unraveling fast.

## Job #13: Trade Show Setter Upper – Age 22 – 1986

I got the job the way I got a lot of jobs back then, through a friend. He was already working for **U-Neek Display**, setting up trade show booths in and around Washington, DC, and he didn't mind me tagging along as long as I could pitch in. I didn't have a car, so I was chained to his schedule: if he worked, I worked. If he didn't, I stayed home. In total, I probably only managed a dozen gigs, each one sandwiched between whatever other jobs I was juggling at the time.

These were the years when I was a functioning junkie. Mornings had their ritual: just enough to steady myself before heading out, so I could make it through a workday without collapsing into sweats and cramps. A little to keep the sickness down, but never enough to really quiet the craving. That was reserved for when I made it back home, when I could do it "right." In between, I moved through life like a man holding a wolf by the ears... working, talking, joking, while always aware of the beast waiting to tear loose.

The job itself was muscle work. Unloading crates, bolting together aluminum frames, carpeting over cement floors, hanging banners that promised a shinier future than the ones most of us were living. Convention centers were all the same --- cavernous echo chambers filled with the honking of forklifts, the sour stink of perspiration mixing with the artificial new-carpet smell, union guys bitching about hours before we'd even had coffee. The suits who'd later strut in with their brochures and rehearsed smiles never thought about who laid the foundation. We were the ghosts that built their stage, sweating through our shirts while they planned their product launches.

What I remember most wasn't the work, though. It was the truck driver. An older Black man, tall and wiry, with skin worn to leather and a cowboy hat fused to his head like it had grown there. Cowboy boots too, clicking across the concrete as if he'd just stepped out of a Western. He'd roll in with a load, lean against the trailer, and suddenly the loading dock turned into a saloon, him the gunslinger holding court.

He spun his past into legends. Nights spent sleeping in a hammock strung under his trailer, the ground shifting beneath him like waves. Fires built roadside, beans and meat sizzling in a cast-iron pan while rigs roared past in the dark. He told of women who came and went, fights that broke out over whiskey, mornings spent hungover but alive, staring down another hundred miles with nothing but blacktop and sky ahead. To him, trucking wasn't a job. It was the last outlaw trade, the diesel horse under him and the highway his open prairie.

I don't know how much of it was true. Probably half at best, but truth wasn't the point. His stories lifted the grind out of the dust and noise. While we were bolting aluminum poles and unrolling corporate carpet, he was dragging us into a world that was raw and romantic, dangerous and free, where life was lived by firelight and asphalt.

I can't tell you what companies I built booths for, or what hollow slogans we stapled up to the rafters. That's all gone. But I can still see that trucker, skinny frame wrapped in leather and denim, boots clicking, hat shadowing his eyes, standing tall against the chaos, spinning tales of the road like the last cowboy holding out against the death of the Wild West.

## Job #14: Food Runner/Busboy – Age 22 – 1986

This was one of those "only when desperate" gigs --- the kind that doesn't define you, doesn't even really feed you, but keeps the lights on just long enough to stumble into the next chapter. My friend Keith, a fellow survivor from the Museum Café trenches, had leveled up. He was now managing and bartending at **Pacifica Restaurant**, and every so often he'd call me like a fireman ringing the alarm bell: short-staffed, slammed, chaos in the dining room. "Can you come in and help me out?" If I could stand upright and find a clean shirt, I was in.

Pacifica was trendy for its time, a West Coast import in a city that still fancied itself more hot dogs and Natty Boh than mesquite smoke and shrimp skewers. Their whole shtick was the grill --- mesquite grilled everything, the smoke pouring out like incense, branding the food with a flavor that was primal, almost violent. Shrimp were the star, charred and sweet at the same time, and I inhaled them whenever they came my way. That smoke clung to your clothes like a jealous lover, followed you home, into bed, into your dreams.

The restaurant had two dining rooms --- one tucked downstairs, cozy and loud, the other perched upstairs, reached by a winding staircase that felt more like a booby trap than an architectural choice. Carrying heavy trays up that thing was like running an obstacle course blindfolded. The stairs were narrow, the turn sharp, and just when you had momentum, a customer would come down in your path, and you'd have to swerve or risk dumping mesquite-grilled dinner into their lap. Every trip was a gamble --- one misstep and the night's profit became a heap of rubble at the bottom of the staircase.

I didn't work there often. A handful of shifts, really. The details blur together, probably because this was deep in the fog years, when my addiction had turned days into greasy fingerprints on glass --- you knew something had happened, but you couldn't see it clearly. The work was simple: clear the tables, run the plates, smile when you had to. Go home with a couple bucks in your pocket and the same hunger gnawing at your ribs.

What stands out isn't the food or the customers, it's the theater of deception I carried everywhere. By then, I'd become an Olympic-level liar. Girlfriends didn't know. Family didn't know. Friends didn't know. To them, I was just Peter hustling jobs like always, filling shifts, bouncing between kitchens, scraping together a living. Only the dealers and the users knew the real story. Everyone else got the polished version --- the show.

So Pacifica was another stage, another mask. Upstairs or downstairs, I was a busboy, grinning, sweating, hustling food between tables like any other young guy trying to make rent. Behind the scenes, I was already calculating, scheming, hiding. Every "How's it going?" from a coworker was just another line to deliver. "Good, man. Busy. You know how it is." And then back to stacking plates, clearing crumbs, keeping the act together.

Keith lived in Charles Village, not far from the apartment I shared with my roommate, Peter. That little overlap of geography made the calls easy, the work accessible. But nothing about Pacifica stuck with me the way other jobs did. It was filler, mesquite smoke and staircases, a side hustle in the middle of my secret war.

Some jobs mark you, leave scars, tattoo themselves into your memory. Pacifica didn't. It slid by in the haze --- another night, another dollar, another round in the quiet theater of keeping myself together just long enough to fall apart again.

**Job #15: Waiter – Age 23 – 1987**

**Petro's** was a Greek restaurant I landed in thanks to a neighborhood connection. Art and Maria, the owners, had lived just a block from me when I was a kid, so by the time I walked in asking for work, they already knew who I was. That familiarity was enough to get me hired, first as a waiter, sometimes slipping into the kitchen on slow afternoons to chop, prep, and watch the rhythm of a cuisine I barely knew.

Until then, Greek food was little more than gyros from Lexington Market or something I might stumble on at a street festival. At Petro's, I fell in love with it. Moussaka stacked like edible architecture, avgolemono soup that punched and soothed at the same time, and baklava sticky enough to glue your fingers together. But the thing that hooked me hardest was Greek coffee. Jet black, thick enough to chew, with grounds that clung to your teeth, and a caffeine hit that could light up your skull. I learned to make it there, and it became a ritual, a small ceremony I carried with me long after the job itself vanished.

One of my coworkers, a Middle Eastern guy whose name I can't recall, gave me one of the best cultural shocks of my life. We'd sneak out after shifts, and he'd always have the best hash. One night, he told me that in his village every house kept a supply of it. Like bread, like tea. When you visited, hash was offered as naturally as water, and refusing it was considered rude. That floored me. Drugs, to me, had always been something hidden, whispered, concealed. To him, it was hospitality, no different than passing the salt. It made my own relationship to it feel both darker and smaller.

But while Petro's gave me new flavors, my personal life was collapsing. By then I was living in a crumbling South Baltimore rowhouse with Yuri, the Russian artist I'd met at the Howard Room. Four bedrooms for dirt cheap, but what I really bought was isolation. The house was falling apart, and so was I.

One morning I woke up on a mattress on the floor, sick, covered in vomit, my body wrecked. I glanced at the clock, realized I was late for work, and called Petro's to explain. That's when they blindsided me. "Why didn't you show up yesterday?" they asked. Yesterday? I had no memory of missing a shift. Somewhere in that haze, I must have overdosed, passed out, and slept through an entire day. The thought chilled me to the bone. I could have died in that filthy room, and no one would have known until the stench gave me away.

Petro's fired me on the spot, but that wasn't the real consequence. The real hit was the realization of just how far gone I was.

Terrified, I called my father. For the first time, I admitted I needed help. I told him I had been using cocaine, too ashamed to say the word heroin out loud. He didn't hesitate. He picked me up, no judgment, no lecture, just a father grabbing his son before he disappeared for good. I threw everything I owned into a duffel bag and walked out of that rowhouse, leaving Yuri, the mattress, and the wreckage of that life behind.

The next week was spent in my old bedroom, riding out withdrawal cold turkey. It was hell. No medical detox, no counselors, just sweat, shakes, and a clock that refused to move. But it was also the end of my heroin use. Not the end of my addictive nature --- that beast would find other outlets --- but it was the first time I'd drawn a line in the sand.

Petro's was supposed to be just another job. Instead, it became the place where I saw how close I was to losing everything. A restaurant full of new flavors and old rituals, and behind it all, a breaking point I couldn't ignore.

## Job #16: Gas Station Attendant – Age 23 – 1987

Still living at home, still trying to figure out what the hell
I was doing with my life, I landed a job at the **Guilford
Exxon** up in Roland Park. It lasted only a few months, but
in that short stretch I found myself working in what was
probably the last full-service gas station in Baltimore, a
museum piece disguised as a business.

Full service meant just that. Customers never had to step
out of their cars. We pumped the gas, cleaned the front
and rear windshields, checked the tire pressure, and
delivered the ritual question: "Check da ool?"
Baltimorese for, "Would you like me to check your oil?"
It rolled off our tongues like a chant, as natural as the
smell of gasoline in the air. They paid extra for the
privilege, one gallon at a time, and in return we
performed like a pit crew with manners.

I wasn't alone in it. My brother Joe worked there, along
with Boo and Chris, a couple of guys I'd grown up with.
Having them around made the place feel like a reunion of
sorts, like we'd all been sucked back into the same orbit
after drifting. It wasn't glamorous work, but there was a
comfort in standing side by side with people who knew
where you came from.

The real soul of the place, though, was Big Lou. He was
the mechanic, always wedged under a hood or sprawled
under a chassis, his hands black with grease that never
quite washed off. Lou didn't say much, but when he
barked for a wrench, you moved. If business was slow,
we pitched in, holding parts, steadying tailpipes, fetching

tools, learning little tricks from him without realizing we were getting an education.

And then there were the tires. Fixing flats was the goldmine. Four or five bucks a pop, and we got to keep the cash. Every time someone limped in with a nail stuck in the tread, we pounced. Patching rubber, banging out rims, balancing tires on old machines that rattled like carnival rides --- we did it all, greasy and grinning because the payoff was immediate. In a world of hourly wages, those fives felt like winning scratch-offs.

We had our share of memorable customers, but none bigger than Oprah Winfrey. Back then she was still a Baltimore news anchor, not yet the global empire, but she carried herself like she already knew where she was heading. She pulled in, we went through the same motions we did for everyone else, and that was the point --- no fanfare, no snapping to attention, just another car at the pump. Maybe that's what made it cool. Oprah got the same "check da ool?" treatment as the accountant in a Corolla or the housewife in a station wagon. Equal parts Baltimore respect and Baltimore indifference.

Most days blurred together, the smell of gas and oil soaking into my clothes, but one afternoon blew the doors off routine. My buddy Greg pulled in, riding shotgun in a beat-to-hell VW bug. We shot the usual greetings, and then he leaned over and asked, "You want any MDMA?"

I blinked. "What the hell is that?"

"Kinda like acid, but lighter. Just try it." He pressed two capsules of white powder into my hand.

"What do I do with these?"

"Crack 'em open, dump 'em in some water, drink it down." Then he was gone, as casual as if he'd just offered me gum.

So I did.

Not long after, the whole world lit up. My body hummed like an electric wire. Energy, euphoria, and a sudden surge of horniness like I'd never known came crashing in all at once. Suddenly the full-service ritual had a whole new undertone. "Check da ool?" sounded like a pick-up line. Every windshield sparkled like crystal; every customer's face glowed like they'd been lit by Hollywood spotlights.

I was buzzing so hard I could barely keep my hands steady, and when they did steady, they were still smeared with grease. That kept me from disappearing into the bathroom for a little "private relief," but the thought hung in the air, throbbing along with the chemical high.

Guilford Exxon wasn't just a gas station. It was a combustion chamber --- not just for cars, but for people. You could pull in for fuel and end up with a front-row seat to your future, your friends, or the unexpected euphoria of powder in a capsule. Gas, oil, grease, and MDMA --- that's what fueled me, at least for one unforgettable day.

## Job #17: Communications Department – Age 23 – 1987

My mom worked in the Dean's office of the Continuing Education Department at **Johns Hopkins University,** and she managed to get me an interview. Nepotism, pure and simple. That's how I wound up in the Communications Department at one of the most prestigious universities in the country, wearing thrift store slacks and trying to look like I belonged.

I only stayed about a month. The work wasn't hard, but it was soul-numbing. Most of it was sending and receiving faxes --- the pinnacle of high technology in 1987 --- and wrestling with DOS commands on sleek new computers that felt like something out of Tron. They hummed, beeped, and blinked like they were solving the world's problems, but all I was doing was routing other people's memos.

The department itself was buried in the basement, fluorescent tubes buzzing overhead, the air a little too dry, a little too still. It was less ivory tower and more holding pen for academic misfits. A handful of us sat in that bunker, shuffling papers, pretending to look purposeful while time dragged like a bad hangover. Johns Hopkins on the letterhead, sure, but the vibe was closer to jury duty.

The highlight of my day had nothing to do with the job. It was lunch with my mom. Every so often we'd meet in one of the cafeterias, and for half an hour I could forget the humming machines and the subterranean gloom. I loved everything about those cafeterias: the steam trays lined with choices, the metal rails under my plastic tray, the small thrill of being able to pick whatever I wanted. Fried chicken one day, lasagna the next, pudding cups lined up like tiny rewards for surviving adulthood. And best of all, Mom always paid. For a broke kid still patching up the wreckage of heroin, it was a little oasis.

Meanwhile, I had applied to Towson State University. My parents pushed hard for me to go to college, and though my heart wasn't in it, I was out of ideas in my post-heroin, trying-to-stay-straight phase. Philosophy and art classes sounded like they might point me toward something that wasn't just another job with a timecard and fluorescent lighting.

After a month of faxes, DOS prompts, and the buzzing drone of a basement office, I was done. I walked away from Johns Hopkins and tried my hand at being a student. It wasn't passion, exactly --- more like grasping at something, anything, that felt like a step forward.

### Job #18: Catering Server/Bartender – Age 23 – 1987

I started working with a company called **Selective Servers**, which supplied staff for high-end events. It was an easy fit, I had formal dining experience, and I still owned a couple of tuxedos left over from my days in the John Eager Howard Room. Best of all, the work was flexible. I could pick up shifts when it suited me and skip them when it didn't.

On the bigger events we did in DC, and there were a few, we'd all meet at the office in Baltimore and then get bussed down together in a rented charter. It made things easy---no worrying about traffic, no trying to figure out parking, just hop on and ride straight to the loading dock or service entrance. Plus, the charter came with a restroom on board, which was no small perk when you'd been standing around in a tux since mid-afternoon.

One of the most memorable gigs was a massive fundraising dinner for the Republican Party at a convention center in Washington, DC. Ronald Reagan himself was there, along with a parade of political heavyweights. Each server was assigned to a single table of eight, and I was told that guests had paid thousands of dollars apiece to attend.

The dinner was served French-style, which was fine by me. I'd already mastered the one-handed fork-and-spoon technique, the kind of muscle memory that made plating food at the table look effortless. I placed each portion cleanly onto plates, just the way it was supposed to be done. A lot of the newer servers hadn't learned the finesse yet, and they dive-bombed portions onto plates from above, meat and potatoes landing with a thud like mortar shells. It wasn't graceful, but nothing ever hit the floor. Guests winced, but the show went on.

Security was everywhere. Secret Service agents stood like statues at every corner, eyes scanning constantly. Upon arrival, we were each issued a serving fork and spoon, tools of the trade. At one point, I reached into my inside breast pocket to retrieve mine, and a Secret Service agent appeared instantly, materializing out of nowhere, ready to intervene if what I pulled out wasn't cutlery.

As I moved between tables, balancing trays and scanning for cues, my mind started to wander. I pictured what would happen if I suddenly bolted toward the stage, straight at Reagan and his entourage. How far would I get? Would they tackle me mid-stride, or would I make it all the way to the spotlight before being taken down?

Of course, I kept my fantasies to myself, smiled politely, and went back to serving plates. But for a few seconds, standing in a tuxedo with a fork and spoon in hand, I imagined myself not just part of the event, but part of history, however brief and disastrous that history might have been.

The other perk of these kinds of events was what came after the dinner service. Once the guests were fed, we were often allowed to eat the leftovers --- filet mignon, prime rib, and all the fixings. For someone living day to day, sometimes not sure where the next decent meal was coming from, that was a big-time benefit. On more than one occasion, I walked away from a high-society wedding or political fundraiser with a belly full of food I could never have afforded on my own.

## Job #19: Events & Conference Services – Age 23 – 1987

While taking classes at **Towson State University**, I picked up a summer job with the Events & Conference Services Department. Since the high-rise dorms weren't being used by students, we ran them like hotels. Families, athletes, academic groups, you name it --- if they booked space on campus, we were the ones handing out keys and making sure the rooms were flipped between stays.

The work itself was straightforward. Beds stripped and remade, trash out, bathrooms wiped down, toiletries lined up like we were prepping for a hotel inspector. The front desk was its own performance: smile, hand over the keys, give directions to elevators that clanked and groaned like they'd been built before the war. It was grunt work, but it came with a perk that mattered more than money: free room and board. For a guy who'd spent the last few years in rowhouses and basements, moving into a dorm and sliding a tray through the cafeteria line felt like I'd stumbled into a version of the "college experience" I'd mostly skipped.

The biggest event of the summer was hosting the Special Olympics. For a week, the dorms were alive with energy --- athletes, families, volunteers, coaches, everyone buzzing through the halls. Elevators crammed with wheelchairs and crutches, laughter echoing off the concrete stairwells, kids high-fiving at the front desk like they'd just won gold. By the end, the cleanup was heavier than usual --- laundry bags overflowing, toothpaste smeared across mirrors, and snack wrappers jammed into drawers was the least of it --- but none of it felt like a burden. The atmosphere those guests brought with them stuck around long after they checked out.

Off the clock, we were allowed to use the facilities like paying students. Pools, tennis courts, basketball courts, the weight room --- all available, it felt like a gift. We were a little tribe of summer staff with access to buildings that technically weren't ours, drifting between shifts and pick-up games, cafeteria meals and front desk rotations.

Most of the names faded after that summer, blurred into the churn of jobs and moves that came later. But one stayed: Carlton. He was easygoing, funny, always messing with the radio at the front desk, always quick with a joke when the monotony started to choke the air out of the room. Before we parted ways, he handed me a mixtape he'd put together. Run-DMC, The Fat Boys, Grandmaster Flash, the whole scratch-and-boom of the era crammed onto one cassette.

That tape still lives in a box somewhere, plastic scuffed, the handwriting fading. Whenever I dig it out, I'm pulled back to that Towson summer --- the smell of cafeteria coffee, the hum of fluorescent lights in the front desk lobby, the dorm halls rattling with athletes during the Special Olympics. For a few months, I wasn't just working. I was orbiting around something that felt like college, even if it wasn't really mine.

## Job #20: Knife Salesman – Age 23 – 1987

It started by accident. I wasn't looking for a job. I was cutting through the Student Union on my way to the arcade, quarters in my pocket, eyes on the glowing promise of Galaga, when I stumbled into a career fair. Ninety percent of the booths looked like hell on earth --- suits, briefcases, pamphlets promising "opportunity." But one stopped me cold, **Cutco Cutlery**: a table lined with knives. Not just any knives. Gleaming, stainless steel, handles polished like piano keys. After my time chopping vegetables and filleting trout in kitchens, I couldn't resist.

I signed up for an interview on the spot. The next thing I knew, I was sitting in a room with a handful of other suckers, watching a slick young recruiter slice tomatoes into translucent sheets, like origami made out of produce. Then came the kitchen shears --- the big finale --- cutting a copper penny in half as if the laws of metallurgy had taken the day off. By the end, we weren't just impressed. We were drafted.

"Extensive training" turned out to be memorizing a script and practicing our best smile in front of a mirror. They called it direct sales; I didn't know the term "multi-level marketing" yet. What it meant in practice was this: I had to buy my own demo kit, carry it everywhere, and sell knives to anyone foolish enough to let me through the door.

My first victims were, of course, my parents. They bought a few pieces out of love or pity, maybe both. One of my grandparents caved too, springing for the miracle shears. That was the high-water mark of my sales career.

After that, it was desperation. I hauled my kit back to the Museum Café, thinking maybe my old boss would spring for a set. I gave him the full pitch: the tomato trick, the penny shear stunt, the sales smile that felt like it was stapled to my face. He sat through the whole thing politely, arms folded, waiting for the big finish. When I sliced the penny, he nodded once and said, "That's neat. But I don't really need to cut pennies in half." That was the end of the pitch, and the end of the sale.

By the time the shine wore off, I realized I'd blown money I didn't have on a kit I couldn't unload. The knives themselves were solid --- no joke about that. Cutco made quality. My mom still has some of the set I sold her, pushing forty years later. That's a better track record than most marriages. But me? I wasn't cut out for knife evangelism. I didn't have the shark grin or the endless optimism it took to keep knocking on doors and pretending every housewife secretly dreamed of julienning tomatoes so thin you could read a newspaper through them.

What I walked away with wasn't money. It was the memory of standing in strangers' kitchens, cutting up their produce like a lunatic, pitching miracle steel with a desperation that reeked of both cologne and fear. My first tango with the world of pyramid schemes disguised as opportunity, and I walked out poorer, wiser, and still with a set of knives that never let me forget it.

## Job #21: House Painter – Age 23 – 1987

Scott and Tom called it a painting company, but really it was two guys with ladders and a beat-up pickup, trying to hustle their way into Roland Park money. Scott was the brother of the singer in my brother's band, and Tom was a guy I'd done more than a little cocaine with over the years. Not exactly Sherwin-Williams' A-team. They needed help, I needed cash, so I said yes.

The houses we painted weren't the storybook Roland Park mansions you see in postcards --- not anymore. These were the ones chopped into apartments, sagging porches, window frames soft as bread. Once, they'd been architectural flexes, proof a man had "made it." By the time we showed up, they were carcasses being whitewashed for another decade of cheap rent.

There was no prep work. None. Forget scraping or sanding. Forget fixing the rotted putty or the termite-gnawed trim. We painted right over the sins --- dirt, bugs, peeling flakes that curled like old scabs. The brush picked up whatever was in its way, mashed it into the siding, sealed it under another skin of latex. From the sidewalk, it looked fine. Up close, it was a crime scene with primer.

Scott and Tom loved the idea of owning a painting business more than the reality. On site, it was chaos: ladders leaning at drunken angles, buckets tipped over in the grass, tarps bunched in the corners like dirty laundry. We'd half-finish a house, disappear for two days, and come back to an owner red-faced on the porch demanding to know if we'd ever return. Sometimes we did. Sometimes we cracked beers at noon, splattered each other with paint, and let the job drift away in a haze.

Money was hand to mouth, literally. Cash in a palm at the end of the day, enough to buy a six-pack, a bag of weed, and some Chinese takeout if you were lucky. I didn't care. It was summer work, nothing more. A way to kill the hours while the rest of my life felt like a stalled engine.

At the same time, I was making promo posters for my brother's band. Collages of clip art, layers on layers, text cut and pasted until it looked less like a flyer and more like a ransom note with rhythm. They weren't jobs --- nobody paid me for them --- but they felt like work, creative work, in a way that painting houses never did. The posters had style, and in a world of Xeroxed garbage stapled to poles, mine stood out.

The painting gigs, though? They were a joke. But sometimes a joke puts cash in your pocket. And sometimes that's all you need.

### Job #22: Cook – Age 23 – 1987

By this point, I'd moved back out of my parents' house. I was juggling classes at Towson with a grill cook gig at **Alonso's** in Roland Park --- the kind of neighborhood joint where the regulars knew each other's orders by heart and the main attraction was a culinary abomination disguised as a bragging right: the two-pound hamburger. They called it the Meal in a Basket.

This thing wasn't a burger so much as a dare wrapped in wax paper. A stunt food before stunt food became a marketing strategy. Nobody in their right mind would cook a two-pound burger to order, so we rigged the system. Half-cooked patties were par-cooked on the grill, stacked like greasy bricks in a bus tub, and slid under the oven on the line to keep warm in their own fat. When someone actually ordered one, we'd pull out a semi-congealed slab, slap it back on the grill, and pretend it was freshly cooked. The whole process smelled like a gym sock left in bacon grease. I wouldn't have touched one on a dare, let alone paid for it.

The kitchen itself was a shoebox. Barely enough space to turn without elbowing the fryer or knocking over the pizza station. For lunch shifts, I ran it solo --- one man against the tide, trying to keep up with orders while the sweat dripped down my neck and onto the griddle. Dinner was at least two cooks, but even then it was a knife fight against the tickets, the kind of scramble that made you feel like you were drowning in grease and chatter.

The pizzas were another "specialty." Store-bought frozen crusts that came in blank disks, more factory than food. We tried to compensate with sheer volume --- toppings piled so high you half expected the tower to collapse in transit. Order a pepperoni, and you got PEPPERONI, a pepperoni landslide that made the crust an afterthought. People loved it. In Roland Park, excess sold better than craft.

The bar stayed busy, the kind of place where afternoons bled into nights and nobody looked at the clock. Mugs clinked, smoke hung in the air, and the chatter from the regulars was as constant as the hiss of the fryer. The owner, whose name I can't for the life of me remember, spent most of his time lurking in the basement, a dungeon that reeked of stale beer and mildew. He'd pop up occasionally to survey the crowd, then vanish back down like a mole returning to its hole. The place ran on its own momentum.

For me, Alonso's was a weird kind of full circle. Just a few blocks up from Guilford Exxon, where I'd pumped gas and checked "da ool," I was now slinging grease-soaked pizzas and reviving half-dead hamburgers for the same neighborhood. By day I was a half-interested college student; by night, a short-order survivor in a sweatbox kitchen that never slowed down.

### Job #23: Bartender – Age 23 – 1987

An old girlfriend who had gone off to college called me out of the blue. Her dad, Bill, had just bought a bar in Fells Point and needed bartenders. I'd poured drinks at catering gigs, sure, but never in a real bar, with real regulars who staked their lives around the same stool every night. Two days later, I was behind the taps at **The Wharf Rat**.

Before Bill, The Wharf Rat had been infamous --- locals only, outsiders keep out. The staff wore T-shirts with the slogan stamped across the chest: Better a Wharf Rat's Darling Than a Preppy's Slave. Bill wanted none of that baggage. He scrubbed the logo, softened the image, and tried to make the place more welcoming. He also brought his own tastes into the beer program. Long before "craft beer" was a household phrase, we were pouring what I'd now call first-wave microbrews --- Clipper Brewing, Sam Adams --- alongside the everyday standards. Later, after I was gone, Bill went further and started Oliver Brewing, but even then you could see the ambition bubbling up in the tap lines.

The actual day-to-day was simpler: pour beers, swap stories, keep the peace. What set the place apart was the giant barrel of popcorn parked in front of the bar. Free, always overflowing, refilled until the last stragglers staggered out at closing time. People tore into it like raccoons in a dumpster, salt crusting their lips and oil on their fingers. For plenty of regulars, that barrel wasn't just a snack --- it was dinner. A pint of Clipper or Boh and a mountain of popcorn could carry someone straight through to last call.

I had my own little trademark back then --- the beret. I wore it everywhere, part punk, part art-student, part whatever character I thought I was playing. Before long, the rest of the staff started wearing them too. Eventually, Bill had Wharf Rat berets made up and sold them along with the T-shirts. I went from just being the new bartender to being a trendsetter without even meaning to.

Outside, Fells Point was still rough, still real. Developers hadn't polished it yet. It was cobblestones, sagging rowhouses, and more bars per block than made sense. They said it was the densest drinking neighborhood in the country, and walking those streets, you believed it. Every doorway hid another tavern, each with its own lifers, drifters, and corner philosophers.

For me, The Wharf Rat was the perfect fit. It was a stage where I could bartend, party, and burn the candle from both ends. By then, heroin was behind me, but everything else was fair game --- booze, weed, mushrooms, whatever was within arm's reach. I was riding my motorcycle year-round, even in Baltimore winters, parking out front and stepping behind the bar still smelling like exhaust and cold air.

School was slipping further out of sight. The bar world had its claws in me now --- neon lights, jukebox shadows, popcorn barrels, berets behind the taps, and early craft beers pouring from the lines. Looking back, it was the crossroads of two worlds: the last of the old Fells Point and the very first stirrings of the craft beer revolution.

### Job #24: House Painter – Age 23 – 1987

While working at The Wharf Rat, I fell in with another bartender we all called Big Rick. The nickname wasn't irony --- the guy was a walking redwood, close to seven feet tall, with a mustache thick enough to smuggle contraband and the kind of rugged good looks that made him look like Tom Selleck's taller cousin. He had the build of a guy who once had big dreams on a basketball court, and the limp of a man whose knee had betrayed him.

Bartending was his night job. His real hustle was during the day, running a legit painting business. Rick wasn't just slapping paint on walls. He took pride in it --- clean lines, proper prep, the kind of work that had high-dollar homeowners handing over their keys. Every so often, he'd let me tag along for extra cash, a sidecar on his steady gig.

The houses were nothing like the rowhomes I grew up around. These were the big Roland Park and Guilford addresses --- old money mansions with trimmed hedges, stone walkways, and landscaping that had probably cost more than any house I'd ever lived in. Everything had that suffocating neatness that told you someone's gardener had a tighter schedule than you did.

One afternoon, I was up on a ladder painting trim around a set of second-story windows. It was one of those hot Baltimore days when the humidity stuck to your skin like an extra layer of clothes. Sweat dripped into my eyes, my arms were shaking, and instead of doing the smart thing --- climbing down, moving the ladder, climbing back up --- I went for the big stretch. Everyone who's ever worked a ladder knows that stretch. The stupid, cocky reach for "just one more brush stroke" that almost always ends badly.

The ladder tilted. Gravity laughed. And in a blink, I was airborne, clutching the bucket like a cartoon character before both of us went headfirst into the bushes below.

I got lucky. The ground didn't break me, and the ladder missed my skull by inches. But the bush --- oh, the bush. It wasn't just a bush. It was a shrine to wealth and patience; one of those fifty-year-old foundation shrubs sculpted into perfection by decades of gardeners with clippers. Now it looked like modern art. A leafy Jackson Pollock, dripping in white paint.

Rick wasn't amused. His mustache twitched, his face tightened, and I could practically hear his knee screaming from beyond the grave. He didn't yell. He didn't need to. The silence was worse.

I spent the rest of the day --- and the next --- on my knees, working leaf by leaf, wiping paint with rags, solvents, and whatever desperate tricks Rick could think of. It was tedious, humiliating, and utterly hopeless. The plant survived, but it never looked the same.

Rick eventually forgave me. Maybe because he knew I'd learned the hard way. Or maybe because he figured the universe had already punished me enough --- hours on my knees, dripping in the sun, apologizing to a shrub. Either way, the lesson burned itself in: ladders don't forgive shortcuts, and in the world of the wealthy, their shrubs are practically family.

**Job #25 – Taxi Driver – Age 23 – 1987**

At the time, I didn't own a car, just a motorcycle with a personality disorder. The wiring was fried, the battery unreliable, and I carried a little charger in my backpack like a life-support machine. Practical? Not at all. That's how I ended up renting my wheels from **Arrow Cab**

**Company** --- white taxis with green lettering, ex-police cruisers and tired sedans beaten to hell, patched together just enough to keep rolling.

Arrow's deal was straightforward extortion: pay them $85 for a 12-hour shift, cover your own gas, and pray you pulled in enough fares to make it worth it. Most days I did the math --- once the nut was covered, I drove the cab like it was my personal car. Errands, food runs, joyrides. It was cheaper than owning a beater.

Baltimore at night was the real theater. The back seat filled with bar drunks, working girls, and suits with the stink of someone else's perfume. But the ride that branded itself into memory came near the end of one shift.

It was about 11 p.m. and I had decided to call it and early night, when a guy waved me down outside a bar. I figured what the hell. He was the bartender and said that one of his regulars needed a ride home. He said she only comes in once a month but has been doing it for many years. She was in her seventies or so, dolled up in pearls and a dress better suited for cocktails at the country club than last call in the city. The alcohol fumes hit first, then her shrill command.

"HOME!" she barked.

"Right," I said. "Where's home?"

She blinked, eyes swimming, and shouted: "I DON'T KNOW, YOU'RE THE DRIVER!"

At that moment, I knew she was wasted.

GPS didn't exist, and my road atlas was a crumpled mess stuffed in the glovebox. We drove in circles. She'd jolt awake just long enough to scream "DRIVE, DRIVER!" like I was steering a getaway car, then slump over again. The streets she mumbled were nonsense, a grab bag of city blocks and imaginary avenues.

Hours later, a miracle --- she muttered something that stuck, a name that actually matched the county map. I followed the breadcrumbs out of the city, down dark, unfamiliar roads lined with big lawns and brick colonials. When we finally pulled into her driveway, she snapped sober as if someone had flipped a switch. She stepped out gracefully, thanked me like I'd just chauffeured her from the opera, and pressed a wad of bills into my hand.

The meter was near a hundred bucks by then --- a fortune for me in 1987 --- and she tipped on top of it. My single most profitable shift, courtesy of a drunk society matron who couldn't remember her own address.

Arrow Cab was never about steady income. It was survival in a white-and-green jalopy, chasing fares until your ass went numb. But every so often, the city handed you a story, and this one ended out in the manicured darkness of Baltimore County, far from where it began.


**Job #26: Set Painter – Age 23 – 1987**


This gig came through a husband-and-wife team who owned a little company in Fells Point called **Props and**

**Sets** and would come into the Wharf Rat regularly. They were hustling to carve out a corner of the movie business while Baltimore was still cheap and loose. Back then, before the unions really tightened their grip, the industry was a revolving door of oddballs and freelancers --- and if you could paint, build, or at least stay upright on a ladder, you had a shot. They treated me right, paid well for the hours, and made it feel less like day labor and more like being part of something.

The work itself was a crash course in controlled fakery. On Her Alibi, a Tom Selleck movie, I teamed up with Big Rick --- the seven-foot bartender moonlighting as a painter --- and our assignment was to age a brand-new barn into something that looked like it had been around since Lincoln was a kid. We layered paint, scraped it back, sponged in grime, and rubbed actual dirt into the boards. By the end, it looked like a hundred winters had blown through. From ten feet away it read as "authentic," but up close you could smell the fresh lumber under the illusion.

Then there was Clara's Heart, a Whoopi Goldberg film. That one was inside a studio, where we built and painted a full house front from scratch. Framing, siding, paint --- a whole façade conjured up in a warehouse. It looked sturdy in the camera's eye, but if you leaned against it too hard, the whole illusion shook. A Hollywood home built to last exactly one shooting schedule.

What stuck wasn't just the paint under my fingernails but the weird, expensive improvisations. On Her Alibi, the director blew his stack when he saw that the entire caravan of trucks, trailers, and dressing rooms was parked square in the background of his shots. Nobody could move them because of union driver rules. So instead, someone brought in massive trees, dug up from elsewhere, and replanted them in front of the trucks like a living green screen. Movie magic, Baltimore-style.

For me, the sets were less about stardust and more about the quiet satisfaction of being paid decently to make something look real when it absolutely wasn't. Props and Sets gave me a brief window into that strange circus --- and for a few weeks, I felt like I'd slipped behind the curtain without selling my soul to get there.

### Job #27: Bartender – Age 23 – 1987

The **Cat's Eye Pub** wasn't just a bar; it was one of the oldest surviving shrines in Fells Point. Its front door practically coughed you out onto the cobblestones, close enough to the water that you could smell the brine when the tide shifted. Inside, the walls sweated history --- decades of smoke and spilled beer soaked into the wood, the kind of patina you can't fake.

When Kenny, the owner, dropped dead, it felt like the bar itself lost its pulse. Kenny was a biker, a drinker, a walking hurricane of a man who could throw a party on a Tuesday afternoon and make it feel like Mardi Gras. With him gone, the Cat's Eye was suddenly rudderless, trying to float without the mad captain who'd steered it through the decades.

Irish Mike was left to pick up the pieces. He was scrambling to fill the roster. Nobody wanted Sundays. Dead nights, light tips, and the kind of slow burn that could break your spirit behind the bar. But I signed up. Part loyalty to the neighborhood, part ego, part sheer love for that crooked old pub.

My actual stint there was short --- maybe a month or two --- but the Cat's Eye etched itself into me anyway. The Sunday regulars weren't barflies, they were fixtures. Neighborhood locals, bikers, the occasional musician, all clinging to that waterfront like barnacles. They didn't want fancy cocktails or small talk. They wanted whiskey in a glass, beer in a bottle, and someone behind the bar who wasn't going to look at them sideways for drinking alone.

One night a snowstorm rolled in while I was on shift. Through the warped old front windows, I watched the cobblestones vanish under a layer of white, the whole street falling into silence. The harbor shimmered silver, moonlight bouncing off black water while the wind rattled the glass. Inside, the Cat's Eye glowed like a cave --- the clink of ice in glasses, the low murmur of voices refusing to acknowledge the storm. I poured drinks, wiped the bar, and for once, felt like I was tending more than customers. It was almost like I was keeping vigil for the place itself, holding space for a bar that had just lost its patriarch.

The Cat's Eye didn't need me for long. I was just a stopgap until they found someone permanent, another name in the long roll call of bartenders who passed through. But for a handful of Sundays, I was there when the pub was staggering, trying to find its feet again. I didn't save it, didn't change it, but I was part of the bloodstream for a minute, keeping the heart pumping in a joint that was --- and still is --- a piece of Baltimore's soul.

## Job #28: Bartender – Age 24 – 1988

After The Wharf Rat, I drifted a few blocks over to **Wee Peter's Pub**, another corner of Fells Point's labyrinth of bars. Big Rick came with me --- when you're that tall, you go wherever the hell you want to. Wee Peter's was a different beast. Smaller, darker, the kind of dive that smelled of stale beer and steamed shrimp no matter how many mops you ran over the floor. The air itself felt secondhand, thick with cigarette haze from open to close.

During the week it was a slow heartbeat --- neighborhood regulars working their way through six-packs, strangers killing time, a couple of old pool-sharks grinding quarters into the felt. Dartboards thudded, cues cracked, and conversations bled into the music. A rhythm as steady as the tide.

Weekends? A whole other animal. The Green Turtle sat next door, pulling in the suburban preppy crowd like moths to a bug zapper. Once it filled up, the overflow poured into Wee Peter's, and suddenly our quiet locals' joint turned into Thunderdome. Every bartender knows the look --- khakis and polo shirts with vodka-red faces and too much cheap cologne --- suburban warriors convinced they owned the night. Fights broke out over pool table turns, over girls, over nothing at all. I lost count of how many times I had to separate two guys ready to bleed over whose quarter was on the rail. Bathrooms filled with puke, the floor sticky with beer, the whole bar vibrating with bad decisions.

Rick and I made our own sport out of it. Not the most noble kind, either. After hours, we turned that same pool table into battlegrounds of another sort --- a contest to see who could notch more notches on the felt. It wasn't about romance. It was about conquest, boredom, and the reckless hunger of a couple men who thought consequences were for other people. The table saw more action in those times than the darts and cue balls combined.

The strangest night didn't involve fists or sex or cops. It involved a joint I found while sweeping up after closing. Just lying there on the floor like a tip from some stoned patron. I pocketed it, forgot about it, tossed it into a drawer at home. Weeks later, bone dry and desperate, I cracked it open. Looked like bad weed, leafy, green home grown, barely worth the trouble. But I packed it into the bong anyway.

The hits went down rough. Then the floor tilted. My body buzzed like I'd swallowed a live wire. Colors warped. My reflection in the bathroom mirror stared back with eyes that weren't mine --- each pupil tightening, shifting, looking like tiny little assholes staring into the void. I rubbed at them, hard, convinced I could erase the vision. I couldn't. That wasn't weed. That was PCP.

I staggered around the room, every nerve ending a siren, trying to hold onto reality as it slipped through my fingers. It was terror dressed up as euphoria, and it branded itself onto my memory harder than any fight or hookup ever could.

Wee Peter's was already a bar that thrived on chaos --- the preppy spillover, the regulars who didn't flinch at blood on the floor, the dart games that ended with broken glass. But that was what Fells Point really was back then: unpredictable, feral, and just dangerous enough that a joint off the floor might send you into a whole new universe.

## Job #29: Line Cook – Age 25 – 1989

By the time I wound up at **Love's Restaurant**, I'd already dropped out of college and was sketching out a half-baked plan to head west with my buddy Jon. He was working the kitchen at Love's too, which made it bearable. Misery's lighter when you've got someone to laugh with, especially when you're hip-deep in steam tables and gray roast beef.

Love's was a relic, a neighborhood joint clinging to life. The kind of restaurant that used to mean something to the community but now limped along on "blue hairs" who shuffled in for lunch or an early dinner. The whole place felt embalmed in the 1970s. Brown paneling, dim lights, décor that looked like it was bought wholesale from a liquidation sale two decades earlier. If you squinted, it felt less like a restaurant and more like the common dining hall in a retirement home.

The clientele matched the décor. Old couples who'd been eating the same food for half a century and had no intention of switching it up now. Meatloaf, roast chicken, baked potatoes. Nothing spicy, nothing new. Just the safe, starchy taste of routine. I was on the line during lunches, pumping out plates that could've come straight from a church potluck. Jon and I were the young guys in the back, sweating through our shifts while the lifers around us rolled their eyes at our jokes and lit cigarettes on break like they were refueling for another decade.

One afternoon Jon and I tried to put some lipstick on the pig, so to speak. We rolled out a "special" --- poached salmon with dill hollandaise. A little touch of class, at least compared to the industrial pans of mac and cheese and gray gravy. Jon and I actually thought it looked respectable, almost modern. The waitresses, though, knew better. These were tough, middle-aged women who'd been carrying trays longer than we'd been alive. They took one look at the fish, shook their heads, and before walking it out to the floor, they drowned it in tartar sauce.

We protested. "What the hell are you doing? It already has a sauce!"

They didn't even blink. "Our customers won't eat fish unless it's covered in tartar sauce."

And that was Love's in a nutshell. A place where progress came smothered in tartar sauce, because the people in the booths didn't want change, they wanted the same meal they'd ordered since Nixon was in office.

For me, it was never about the food. Love's was a paycheck, a stopgap, something to hold me over until I could split for California. But standing in that time capsule of a dining room, watching plates of salmon get dragged back to the 1950s under a thick white blanket, I knew I couldn't stick around Baltimore much longer. The future wasn't in brown paneling and meatloaf. It was out west, and I was ready to chase it.

## Interlude: Down on the Corner – 1989

When Jon and I finally made it to California, broke but buzzing with the idea of reinvention, we found an apartment in Oakland, perched right on the corner of 32nd and Peralta in Emeryville. The place wasn't much to look at --- cracked plaster walls, thin carpets that smelled like every tenant before us, windows that rattled in their frames whenever a bus coughed by. But rent was cheap, the neighborhood was alive, and we were in California, which meant anything felt possible.

Directly beneath our apartment sat Duck Kee Market, a narrow little Asian market run by an elderly couple who'd been holding down that spot longer than most of the neighbors. It was the kind of shop where you could buy smokes, a soda, maybe a bruised apple if you weren't picky, all while fluorescent lights buzzed overhead like a hive. The couple barely spoke English, but they didn't need to --- their transactions were all nods, gestures, and the soft slap of dollar bills on the counter.

One afternoon I ducked in for cigarettes. While waiting at the register, something on the wall caught my eye. An album cover,  dusty and yellowed from decades of neglect for being too high to reach: Willie and the Poor Boys by Creedence Clearwater Revival. At first it just looked like another piece of random wall clutter, the way corner stores always collect artifacts of someone else's obsession. But then I leaned closer.

The scene hit me like a sucker punch. Four long-haired guys with guitars, standing outside a market, kids dancing around them like the Pied Piper just rolled into town. My brain flickered, then locked in: holy shit. That wasn't just some market. That was this market. Duck Kee. The one I'd just bought smokes from, the one under my apartment.

I asked the woman at the counter, pointing at the cover, "Is that for sale?"

She shook her head firmly, eyes narrowing like I'd just asked to buy a piece of her family's soul. In halting, deliberate English she said, "Twenty years ago, young boys come. They ask, 'Can we take picture?' Then they come back, give us this."

And suddenly it all made sense. Creedence didn't just invent that street corner vibe for the album. They literally set up shop outside Duck Kee, right under where I was now living. My apartment wasn't just another busted walk-up in Oakland. It was stamped into rock and roll history.

I walked out of there with my smokes, the woman's words still bouncing around in my head, and looked up at the corner. Down on the Corner wasn't just a song anymore. It was a place, my place. Jon and I had stumbled into it by accident, and now every time I hit the stoop or walked past Duck Kee's dusty windows, I felt like I was brushing shoulders with ghosts in flannel shirts and work boots, guitars slung low, singing for spare change while kids danced on the sidewalk. I was living on the "down on the corner", corner.

For a broke twenty-five-year-old who'd just fled Baltimore, it was a strange kind of validation. I hadn't just moved west. I'd moved onto the corner that Creedence made immortal.

### Job #30: Assistant Manager – Age 26 – 1990

My first job in California was at **A.J. Scribblers**, a retail clothing store buried inside the San Leandro Mall. Not exactly rock and roll, but it kept the rent paid and gave me an excuse to people-watch from inside the belly of mall culture. The commute was the best part. I could hop on BART, sink into a seat with my Walkman, and soundtrack the ride with a stack of tapes: The Cure, Talking Heads, maybe some Black Flag or Pegboy, if I needed a jolt.

On game days, though, the train became its own circus. Whenever the Oakland Raiders played at the Coliseum, Raider Nation would flood the cars. It looked like a Mad

Max convention on rails --- spikes, skulls, silver-and-black war paint, shoulder pads that looked stolen off an orc army. The air stank of beer and adrenaline. You half-expected someone to light a flare in the middle of the car. And as wild as it was, it still didn't outdo the Deadheads when the Grateful Dead rolled through the same stop. Tie-dye armies, patchouli clouds, barefoot prophets dragging coolers full of cheap beer. Between the two, the Coliseum station was like a rotating freak show of America's tribes, and I got to sit there with my Walkman, grinning into the chaos.

At Scribblers, my title was "assistant manager," but that was just a fancy way of saying I was the guy in charge of running a clothing experiment that looked more like an art class on acid. Scribblers specialized in spin-art fashion. We had racks of oversized T-shirts, leggings, and accessories waiting to be blasted with neon paint in a giant spinning contraption and then baked dry on a conveyor that looked like it belonged in a pizza joint. Every shift smelled faintly of acrylic and scorched cotton.

The real kicker was the customers. Most of them came armed with "color charts" --- personalized style bibles created by image consultants. These weren't just swatches of fabric. They were supposed to be scientific maps of your destiny. "You're a Summer," one chart might declare, with orders to stick to coral and teal. "You're a Winter," another decreed, condemning you to a lifetime of mauve and navy. Some were broken down by season, others by month, and a few by the goddamn day. I had women standing at the counter, sliding laminated charts toward me like holy scripture, whispering, I need something for next Tuesday.

So I'd strap a shirt onto a board, drizzle paint in exactly the right shades, and watch centrifugal force turn it into "wearable art." Half of it looked like a rave had exploded on cotton. The other half looked like a toddler's accident with finger paints. Either way, they loved it.

It was peak mall-era absurdity: neon lights humming overhead, Muzak droning on, teenagers loitering with Orange Juliuses, and me running what was basically a fashion séance. Not predicting the future, just splattering it in coral and teal.

For a while it wasn't bad. It kept me fed, kept me surrounded by the spectacle, and gave me a paycheck for indulging in one of the stranger fads of the late '80s. Scribblers wasn't just a store. It was a weird little temple to the idea that color could save you, confidence could be spun onto fabric, and mall culture would never die.

### Job #31: Landscaper – Age 26 – 1990

After months of folding T-shirts and spinning paint at Scribblers, I traded mall culture for grass stains and exhaust fumes. A guy I met ran a one-man landscaping business --- one pickup truck, a basement office in his parents' house, and more ambition than infrastructure. He needed someone to cover his regular route while he chased new clients, and I needed cash, so I signed on.

Most of the work was residential, mowing tidy suburban lawns, clipping hedges, and blowing clippings into polite little piles. Nothing glamorous, just repetition under the California sun. But sometimes he sent me out to commercial lots, wild stretches of land where weeds grew shoulder-high, thick stalks that rattled like dry bones when the wind kicked up. I'd wade in with a weed wacker, carving through like I was clearing jungle. By the end of the day, my arms would buzz like live wires, my shirt soaked through, and my face caked with dust and green pulp.

Somewhere in the middle of it all, I realized I'd come full circle. My very first job as a twelve-year-old kid in Baltimore had been cutting lawns with an old push mower, sweating it out for a buck or two from neighbors who thought they were doing me a favor. Back then it was front yards, backyards, broom-swept sidewalks. Now, nearly fifteen years later, here I was again, pushing machines through grass for money. The scale had changed, the tools had changed, but the hustle was the same.

Around that time, I scraped together $500 to buy a Fiat Strada from a guy in Berkeley. The car wheezed like it had emphysema and rattled like loose silverware in a drawer, but it moved, and that was enough. Every morning I'd drive it to my boss's place, leave it parked in front of his parents' house, and swap into his pickup to make the rounds. The Fiat wasn't reliable, but compared to juggling bus routes or depending on BART, it felt like freedom --- if freedom came with balding tires and an exhaust cloud that followed me everywhere.

The hardest part of the job wasn't the mowing or trimming, but finding the damn addresses. This was pre-

GPS, pre-Google Maps. Just scribbled notes on scraps of paper, half-legible directions, and dog-eared maps with coffee stains. More than once I found myself on the wrong side of town, sweating bullets, already behind before I'd even started. By the time I rolled into the right driveway, I was flustered, late, and more worn out than I had any right to be.

Then came the pager. My boss clipped it on me like he was inducting me into the world of professionals. For about a day, I strutted like I'd leveled up. But every buzz meant pulling over, hunting down a payphone, feeding it quarters, and waiting for him to bark an address at me. It didn't take long before the pager felt less like a badge of honor and more like an electronic leash.

Landscaping wasn't a career, not for me, not for the guy who hired me. But it had a strange honesty baked into it. Work in the sun, sweat through your shirt, smell like gasoline and cut grass, then go home with cash in your pocket. I'd started my working life the same way, pushing a mower down cracked Baltimore sidewalks, sweating into my sneakers. Now, a decade and a half later, I was still out there carving grass, chasing the same basic hustle, just with fancier tools and a longer commute.

### Interlude: California Highs – 1990

California was my first taste of weed that deserved a name. Back in Baltimore, what we called "weed" was usually a bag of brittle brown shake, half seeds, half stems, the kind of stuff you had to pick through with tweezers just to get a joint that didn't explode like a sparkler (for the younger readers: seeds explode when you smoke them). It smelled like cut grass and burned like cardboard. Nobody smoked it for the flavor. You smoked it to get sideways and because it was cheap enough that a paper route could cover the cost.

Out west, it was a different religion. The first time I cracked open a bag in Oakland, the air itself seemed to shift. Fat buds, resinous and sticky, glowing green with streaks of purple, sometimes laced with red hairs that looked like veins under skin. One whiff and you knew this was farmed with intent, not scooped off the floor of some dealer's trunk. It came at a price too --- a steep one compared to Baltimore's "downtown brown" weed --- but the high matched the dollar signs. A single hit and the whole city sharpened. The cracked sidewalks looked like veins of a map, the murals popped off brick walls, music on the corner sounded like a live band even if it was just a boom box with tired batteries.

Jon and I knew the first order of business in any new city wasn't finding a bank or a laundromat. It was finding a connection. Oakland was no different. Weed was still illegal, and California cops weren't handing out slaps on the wrist for possession. Getting caught could derail everything before we'd even unpacked. But sobriety wasn't in the cards, so we played the game --- carefully.

Jon somehow lined up a pair of guys in San Francisco, Marcus and Ken. They were our gateway to the good stuff, the kind of dealers who knew the lingo and had the supply to back it up. The trips across the Bay Bridge became routine: scrape together cash, pile into the Fiat, and rattle our way into the city to score. Prices that made us wince, but weed that shut us up quick. Strains with names that sounded like beach towns or sci-fi planets --- Maui Wowie, Northern Lights --- names spoken like passwords that opened a door into another world.

Baltimore weed had always been a whispered transaction, passed in plastic baggies, smoked fast and nervous even in your own home. Out here, it still wasn't above-ground, but it felt elevated. There was a sense of lineage, like every bud had a backstory, a grower, a hillside somewhere kissed by California sun. Smoking it felt like initiation --- a baptism into the West Coast way of doing things.

For me, California wasn't just new jobs, new apartments, new hustles. It was stepping into a city where even the weed felt alive, potent, and mythic. Oakland gave me work and rent headaches. San Francisco gave me Marcus, Ken, and an education in green fire. And somewhere between those Bay Bridge runs and late-night couch sessions, I stopped being a kid scrounging seeds out of a bag and started thinking of myself as a connoisseur.

### Job #32: Warehouse/Delivery – Age 26 – 1990

After sweating through lawns and hedges, I landed at **Such A Business**, the biggest children's general store in the East Bay. They had shops scattered across San Francisco, Berkeley, Oakland, and a couple others, but my world was the Oakland warehouse --- the beating heart where bassinets, cribs, strollers, and stuffed giraffes all piled up before being distributed to the stores or parceled out to families waiting on their "new arrivals."

The warehouse itself was a concrete box with no personality. High ceilings, humming fluorescents, and stacks of cardboard that seemed to breed overnight. My job was equal parts janitor, organizer, and mule. Break down boxes, check incoming shipments, stack things so they didn't fall on your head, and keep the whole chaotic river of baby gear flowing. By then, I'd moved into an apartment on Telegraph Avenue, in the neighborhood called Pill Hill thanks to the fortress of Kaiser Permanente buildings around it. My radius was small, my days routine, but the warehouse kept me moving, sweating, and clocking hours without having to think too much.

A couple times a week, I got paired with another guy for delivery runs. We'd load up a truck with the building blocks of someone's new domestic life --- cribs, dressers, those ridiculous chifferobe changers no one actually needs --- and drive across the Bay to set up entire nurseries in one afternoon. Physically, the work was challenging. But the hardest part was the audience. Nine months pregnant, hormones raging, everything had to be perfect, or you risked a meltdown that made you wish you'd stuck to stacking boxes in Oakland. Screwing in bolts while a woman glared holes through your skull had a way of tightening your nerves.

San Francisco runs were the worst logistically. Tiny streets that looked like they'd been designed for horse carts, hills so steep you prayed the parking brake wasn't lying to you, and delivery addresses that required double-parked heroics in front of honking lines of commuters. But I secretly welcomed those routes. Lunch breaks meant Haight-Ashbury, and Haight meant Rough Trade Records. That place was my church. I'd grab a cheap bite and then spend the rest of the break digging through bins of vinyl and imports you couldn't find anywhere else --- post-punk, obscure indie releases, UK pressings that felt like smuggling contraband back across the Bay.

I'd also picked up a mountain bike, and some mornings I rode it to work. The commute wasn't long, but it was a trip through Oakland's grittier stretches, where street corners were open-air markets of a different sort. One long block along the freeway off-ramps was thick with working girls. They called out to me as I pedaled past in my warehouse clothes, sometimes flashing me like it was all part of the show. Half humor, half hustle. I was just another guy on two wheels cutting through their stage.

One evening the ride paid off in a way that felt like fate tossing me a bone. I spotted a crumpled twenty lying by the curb. I stopped, scooped it up. A few yards later, another. Then another. By the time I'd gathered them all, I had $120 stuffed in my pocket --- a jackpot, almost certainly dropped by some unlucky trucker pulling off the ramp looking to rent some love by the half hour. For me, living paycheck to paycheck, that was like hitting the lottery. I pedaled the rest of the way from work with a grin plastered on my face, lighter than air.

The warehouse job was never glamorous. It was grunt work, sweat, and baby furniture assembly for people I'd never see again. But it gave me small perks: the steady hum of the city around me, vinyl treasures from Rough Trade, and the occasional street miracle like $120 scattered on the asphalt. It wasn't a career, but it kept me fed, moving, and distracted while I stumbled through my own unfinished chapters.

## Job #33: Musician – Age 27 – 1991

After California burned through my pockets and my patience, I came back to Baltimore with a single mission: start a band with my brother, Joe. We wanted noise, proper noise, the kind that made neighbors call cops. So we rented a room at Studio 14, a battered warehouse in a sketchy corner of the city where broken glass glittered like confetti in the gutters and every brick was tagged with someone else's name. Perfect. If your band was going to matter, it had to be born somewhere with rats in the walls and graffiti screaming over your shoulder.

We called ourselves **Jerkwater**, a nod to the trolley line that once rattled up and down the Avenue through Hampden. A name with dirt under its fingernails. A name that already stank of beer, sweat, and working-class defiance. We weren't trying to be clever. We wanted something local, raw, a word you could spit out with a sneer.

I took the reins because someone had to steer the damn ship. I was the one calling clubs, nagging promoters, booking practice time, designing posters, hustling gigs. Joe and I co-wrote the songs --- riffs stitched together with scraps of rage and irony, lyrics scratched out on napkins until they turned into something you could shout into a mic without feeling stupid.

And we were loud. Recklessly, defiantly loud. Other bands rolled in with polite little combo amps, looking to keep things "reasonable." Jerkwater dragged in full Marshall stacks, floor-to-ceiling shrines of wattage. When we hit a chord, it wasn't just heard --- it rattled the cinderblocks, shook dust from the ceiling, and sent muffled complaints bleeding through the hallway. People didn't just know Jerkwater was practicing. They felt it in their ribcages.

Studio 14 was its own jungle. Fifty or so rooms, each packed with another delusion of grandeur. Punk bands pounding out the same three chords like it was a religion. Metal kids chugging riffs so fast the walls sweated. Funk crews hammering grooves until the floor shook. You'd wander the halls like you were walking through a radio dial, every door another station, every room another battle. Bands peeked in on each other --- a nod here, a smirk there --- part camaraderie, part competition. Everybody secretly believed they were the one who was gonna break out, the one who'd get the van, the record deal, the tour.

For five or six years, Jerkwater made Baltimore's dive bars and back-rooms our playground. Load-ins through sketchy alleys, sweat dripping off basement ceilings, soundchecks that never really sounded right. We played to friends, strangers, and occasionally empty rooms, blasting the same songs like they were sermons. And somehow, we even managed a release: a cassette called Updaabenue --- Baltimorese for "Up the Avenue," a wink to Hampden and a middle finger to anyone who thought we were trying too hard.

We got a little digital afterlife too. Our song "Spaceman" still floats around on Spotify, a ghost of that era when we believed --- truly believed --- that Baltimore could be the next Seattle, and we could be the band to lead the charge. Spoiler: we weren't. But back then? Back then we believed enough to shake the walls and sweat through every set like it mattered.

Being a rock star never paid rent, not even close. But it paid in adrenaline, camaraderie, and the raw satisfaction of knowing we were too damn loud to be ignored. And for a while, that was plenty.

**Job #34: Prep Cook – Age 27 – 1991**

When I rolled back into Baltimore, broke but not broken, I picked up a three-month stint at the **Museum Café** --- the same joint where I'd once been dishwasher, prep monkey, and eventually line cook. Years earlier, I'd stormed out in a huff after getting stiffed on a raise. This time, no tantrums, no demands, just a paycheck tied to the Monet exhibit at the Baltimore Museum of Art.

The chef was the same one who'd burned me. We didn't rehash the past. No raised voices about money, no grudges dug up like old bones. He needed hands, I needed work. We let the silence carry it. Outside of work we even found ourselves drinking together, knocking back rounds, chasing white powder, laughing through the kind of late nights that made morning shifts feel like punishment. Strange how time mutates enemies into drinking buddies when you both like to get messy enough.

The job itself was stripped down, mechanical. Croissant sandwiches wrapped in plastic, box lunches lined up like soldiers, salads bagged with packets of dressing rattling around inside. Not real cooking --- more like assembling edible luggage for crowds of Monet pilgrims. The pressure wasn't restaurant chaos anymore. It was production, conveyor belt labor with mayonnaise instead of rivets.

But kitchens never stay clean. One morning I was following the chef around with a notepad, jotting down prep lists, when we stepped into the walk-in. And there he was --- a waiter frozen mid-whippet, can of whipped cream jammed in his mouth, eyes wide like a deer caught in fluorescent headlights. The chef detonated. Fired him right there between the shelves of lettuce and gallon jars of mayo, then muttered something about having just returned a whole case of "defective" whipped cream that mysteriously wouldn't hold its charge. Now he knew why.

The real absurdity wasn't the kitchen. It was the museum itself. A few steps outside the café kitchen, people drifted through hushed galleries, whispering reverently in front of Monet's water lilies, their faces lit like they were witnessing revelations. Meanwhile, I was elbow-deep in tuna salad, bagging up box lunches that sweated in clamshells under fluorescent lights. During breaks I'd sometimes wander into the exhibit, apron still smeared, smelling like onions and cheap vinaigrette, standing among the art lovers who looked at brushstrokes as if decoding the universe. They had Monet --- I had mustard stains.

That collision of worlds stayed with me. In the café, the holy grail was not running out of croissants. In the gallery, it was transcendence by way of impressionist light. At the end of the shift, I didn't smell like linseed oil or oil paint --- I smelled like deli prep. But I still had the luxury of slipping away for a minute, letting the color and light wash over me, before heading back to wrap another sandwich.

Returning to the Museum Café after all those years wasn't nostalgia. It was a loop closing itself, the same chef, the same walk-in, but a different me. Less angry, more tired, strangely at peace with tuna salad and Monet existing under the same roof.

### Job #35: Front of House Manager – Age 28 – 1992

It all started with a bowl of soup. Lisa, my wife at the time, and I ducked into a brand-new café on the Avenue in Hampden for lunch. The neighborhood I'd grown up in was still clinging to its rust and ruin --- pawn shops, dollar stores, boarded windows, and a few greasy carry-outs that could depress even the hungriest stomach. A new sit-down café on 36th Street felt like an alien landing.

Inside, **Café Hon** looked like your grandmother's dining room had been teleported into a Baltimore rowhouse. Lace curtains, mismatched knickknacks, Formica tables with floral designs, and the faint smell of coffee drifting over everything. It was small and cozy to the point of kitsch, but in Hampden back then, kitsch felt revolutionary.

Lisa ordered chicken noodle soup. What landed on the table looked like a biology experiment gone wrong. The noodles had been cooked into oblivion, dissolving into the broth until the bowl was filled with a pale starchy cloud that resembled dishwater more than lunch. We sent it back. The server turned out to be the owner, Denise. Instead of getting defensive, she asked what we would have done differently. Lisa suggested the obvious fix --- cook the noodles separately, add them in to order, don't let them sit and die in the pot. Denise's eyes lit up. "Are you restaurant people?" Within a week Lisa was running the kitchen, and I was in charge of the front of the house.

The timing was perfect. Café Hon was tapping into Baltimore's creative bloodstream at just the right moment. Artists, musicians, misfits --- they embraced it immediately. Hampden locals, not so much. To them it was too "fancy," too weird, too much like Hampden was being invaded by people who used cloth napkins. But the small business crowd got it. The citywide arts scene got it. Even the suburbs came sniffing around, lured in by the promise of "A decent meal for under five bucks." The cheesesteak sub was the priciest item on the menu at $4.95. Everything else was dirt cheap.

But the café wasn't just slinging food. It was pulling Hampden into the future, one egg salad on cheese toast at a time. I started pushing Denise to think bigger --- events, festivals, something to put the Avenue on the map. Hampden's May Fair was tired, a civic hangover no one cared about. Baltimore already had Artscape, SoWeBo, Pow-Wow. Why not Hampden? Plus, my band Jerkwater needed gigs. So Honfest was born --- a neighborhood carnival of hairspray, boas, and beehives. We even ran the Hampden Music and Arts Festival for a couple of years, throwing amplified chaos into the Rec Center where I'd once loitered and played sports as a kid.

Running Café Hon was more than clocking hours. For me, it was personal. I had grown up in Hampden, watching it sag under decades of neglect, always ten steps behind the rest of the city. But I knew its geography made it special. Wyman Park on one side, the Jones Falls on the other --- it wasn't a place you passed through. It was a place you arrived at. That isolation, which once felt like a curse, suddenly felt like an opportunity. Hampden could be its own world if someone gave it a pulse again.

That dingy café with lace curtains and chicken fluff soup gave me a stage. We built something that grew beyond itself, pulled the neighborhood along with it, and cracked open a door to Hampden's revival. I was proud of that.

Still am. Not many people get to look at their childhood streets and say, "Yeah, I helped change this place."

### Job #36: General Manager – Age 30 – 1994

The name was a mistake. The owners had ordered signage and match packs for World Café + Bar, but the printer somehow swapped the plus sign for an X. They didn't bother fixing it. **World CafeXBar** was born, and honestly, the typo fit. The whole place was a happy accident held together with paint, weed smoke, and bravado.

My friend Dave had just signed on as chef. He called me one afternoon: "They're looking for a bar manager. You want in?" I was looking for a change and loved bar life, so I said yes.

The restaurant lived on the second floor of a corner building downtown, a few blocks from the Inner Harbor. To get there, you climbed a long staircase that emptied into a room washed in desert tones and hieroglyph-style murals. Textured canvases leaned on the walls like half-finished dreams, textured fabric panels covered the ceiling catching dim light, and the whole thing looked more like an art installation than a restaurant. It was Baltimore slick --- a little raw, a little crooked, but stylish in its own patched-together way.

The staff was a circus troupe disguised as waiters and bartenders. Musicians, artists, drifters who showed up on time only if the universe allowed it. Somehow, we made it work. Dave could cook his ass off --- his food alone kept the lunch crowd coming back, a mix of lawyers, office workers, and downtown lifers who liked the idea of eating in a place that felt "underground." Dinner was harder. Parking sucked, and people still thought downtown after dark was asking to get mugged. But Dave's food carried us farther than we had any right to go.

There was a tiny upstairs space called the "break room," but nobody ever broke there. It was a permanent hotbox. At any point in a shift, a server would vanish, reemerge twenty minutes later glassy-eyed and stoned, and go right back to hustling tables. Running the place was like herding cats --- if cats were half-baked and wearing aprons.

The ownership was its own soap opera. Four best friends went into business together, which is the restaurant equivalent of playing Russian roulette with five bullets. At first they were all in sync, but the cracks came fast. Arguments over money, ego, control. Eventually three of them pushed the fourth out of his GM role and handed me the keys.

For a while, it felt good. I was running the bar, managing the misfit crew, making deposits every morning like a grown-up. Then one afternoon I checked the account balance and my stomach dropped. Even with the deposit I'd just made, the numbers were circling the drain. The owners weren't reinvesting in the restaurant --- they were siphoning the cash to fund their own lifestyles. The place was bleeding out.

Two weeks without a paycheck was all I could take. I showed up one day, saw the locked doors, and didn't bother opening them. World CafeXBar was dead. The lawsuits came later, angry staff chasing down the wages they'd never see. The murals got painted over, the furniture carted off, the art-dream ambiance dissolved into dust.

For a minute though --- in the haze of the weed room, under those desert murals, with Dave's food hitting the tables and the misfit staff stumbling into rhythm --- it felt like we had built something. And then it vanished, the way most beautiful mistakes do in this business.

### Job #37: General Manager – Age 32 – 1996

After the collapse of World CafeXBar, I wound up back where it had all started: **Café Hon**. Denise had been eyeing an empty space across 36th Street --- bigger footprint, bigger kitchen, bigger possibilities. The kind of move that could either turn a quirky corner café into a Baltimore institution or kill it outright. She told me she wouldn't dare make the jump unless I came back on board. With me running the show out front, she felt like she could risk it. She offered me the General Manager gig. I took it.

The liquor license sealed the deal. I was hungry to build a proper bar program, and take the Café to the next level. We weren't just selling coffee and chicken salad anymore

--- this was about turning the Hon into a full-tilt restaurant and bar.

The move was insane. We closed the doors one afternoon, hauled every stick of furniture, every piece of equipment, and every box across the street, and opened the next day like nothing had happened. It was pure Baltimore scrappiness: no consultants, no corporate logistics team, just a crew of cooks, servers, and friends lugging equipment and everything on dollies across 36th Street while traffic honked around us.

I stayed that night until three in the morning, alone with a roller, slapping paint on the walls so it would look halfway finished when the doors swung open at lunch the next day. My hands were covered in paint, my clothes ruined, but the adrenaline of building something from nothing kept me upright.

The hardest part wasn't the paint or the furniture --- it was the people. The old-school waitresses had been handwriting orders their entire lives. Now I had to strap them into our shiny new POS system, a touchscreen spaceship compared to their order pads. Training sessions felt like hostage negotiations: tears, slammed checks, cigarettes lit mid-shift in the alley while they muttered about "this damn computer." One flat-out refused and I had to create a separate system for her. Most stayed and adapted, grudgingly, their hands hovering over the screens like they might bite back.

We pulled it off. Crowds poured in, the cash register never stopped ringing, and Hampden suddenly had a real player on its hands. But the machine I'd helped build started chewing me up. I was logging brutal weeks, stringing together double shifts, living in the dining room. One morning I hit a wall. Couldn't get out of bed. Couldn't face the bar, the staff, or another lunch rush. I told Denise I was done.

She panicked. Begged me to stay. Offered a tiny raise and, bizarrely, a weekly acupuncture session "to help me relax." I'd lie on a table with needles sticking out of me, wondering how the hell this became part of my GM package. Did it relax me? Not really. But for an hour every week I wasn't being screamed at about a voided ticket or a late food order, and that was enough.

The Café Hon that reopened on the bigger stage wasn't the Café Hon I had signed onto years earlier. The lace-curtain grandma kitchen vibe was gone. In its place was a louder, shinier version of itself --- tourist-friendly, consultant-approved, a little too self-aware. The neighborhood scrappiness that made it special was being traded in for branding, franchising talk, "expansion opportunities." Hampden was changing, and so was the Hon.

I lasted another year. Kept the ship running, trained new staff, kept the bar stocked, nodded along with Denise's ever-bigger schemes. But the spark was gone for me. What had started with a bowl of chicken fluff and a weird little café had grown into a tourist magnet, and I didn't recognize it anymore.

Eventually, I walked away. Café Hon carried on for years, ballooned, imploded, and finally shuttered. For me, it was the end of a personal arc. I'd seen the place in its raw,

experimental infancy and I'd helped it grow into
something bigger than any of us imagined. But the
version I loved --- the off-beat little café where artists,
neighbors, and misfits found their corner --- that place
had been painted over.

## Job #38: Co-Owner, Vintage Clothing Store – Age 33 – 1997

After burning out at Café Hon, I didn't have the stomach
for another restaurant. But Hampden was still calling,
and this time I wanted something I could shape from the
ground up. My old friend Scott --- the same guy I'd once
slung paint with on Roland Park porches --- had been
circling the idea of retail. Together we pulled the trigger
and opened a vintage clothing store on the Avenue. We
called it **Thredhed**. Later it would morph into Galvanize,
but back then it was pure DIY energy, duct tape and
vision.

It wasn't just our shop. We carved the place into sections
and sublet them to other hustlers with their own niche
obsessions. The effect was chaos disguised as commerce.
In the back, a couple offered full-body piercing sessions
like it was the most natural thing to do behind a rack of
polyester bell-bottoms. The basement was claimed by
Son of Reptilian, an offshoot of the infamous Reptilian
Records --- part label, part record store, all noise and
attitude. For a while, one of our street-facing windows
belonged to a woman designing Velcro tear-away dresses
for strippers. Watching her clientele browse in broad

daylight was performance art that doubled as advertising.

The racks upstairs were an unpredictable carnival. Some days it was a flawless pair of mod boots that looked stolen straight from Carnaby Street. Other days it was a disco shirt so loud it seemed to still reek of coke sweat from Studio 54. The unpredictability was the thrill. You didn't shop Thredhed expecting to find something specific --- you came to gamble, to see what the fashion fairies threw your way.

Bands were our bread and butter. With Reptilian Records churning away below, musicians drifted upstairs like smoke. Punk kids, noise bands, indie rockers, all rifling through our racks in search of the thing that would make them pop on stage. A vintage jacket, a pair of pants that didn't look like they came off the sale rack at Gap, a shirt that looked like it had already lived a hundred lives. Thredhed wasn't mall fashion --- it was curated chaos.

Meanwhile, I was feeding another obsession. I'd dropped serious coin on a Power Mac 7200, state of the art at the time, and loaded it with the newest design software. When business was slow, I'd be in the back tinkering with websites, playing with digital collages, teaching myself the language of pixels and code. This was 1997, when most people thought "the internet" was just a myth. But for me it was like discovering another new drug --- only this one let me build worlds instead of burn them down.

And then there was Hilary. She walked in one afternoon looking for piercing jewelry. I was single, restless, maybe cocky, maybe stupid, and I tried a line that should have fallen flat on its face: "Want to model for my webpage?"

Her answer was perfect 1997: "What's a webpage?"

She came back the next day anyway. I shot photos --- racy, playful, nothing polished --- and the chemistry was undeniable. One moment we were strangers in a cluttered vintage shop, the next we were a couple. Twenty-six years later, we still are. Out of all the bizarre subplots of Thredhed, that's the one that mattered most.

The store itself didn't last forever. Hampden was changing, retail was shifting, and eventually the circus moved on. But for a while, Thredhed was a living, breathing crossroads of Baltimore weird: part boutique, part thrift-store roulette, part underground clubhouse, part sideshow. We sold polyester, we hosted noise bands, we watched strippers shop for quick-release dresses, and I found my wife behind the counter.

For a short stretch of time, we weren't just selling vintage clothes. We were selling the experience of stumbling into something raw, strange, and alive.

### Job #39: Freelance Photographer – Age 33 – 1997

Running Thredhed was never going to pay the bills on its own. Vintage polyester and strippers buying Velcro dresses were great for stories, not so great for steady cash. So I hustled wherever I could. One of the stranger side hustles I stumbled into was shooting freelance photography gigs for none other than **Governor William Donald Schaefer**.

By then Schaefer was teaming up with Johns Hopkins on community outreach projects --- ribbon cuttings, fundraisers, neighborhood meet-and-greets, all the soft-focus political theater a career politician needs to stay relevant. And that's where I came in. My job was to float around with a camera and crank out "grip and grin" shots: the governor's hand welded to whoever was in front of him, both of them smiling like their lives depended on it. Ministers, donors, PTA moms, businessmen, kids in Sunday clothes --- click, click, click. It wasn't art, but it was access.

The first time I showed up, I still had my septum ring in. A silver hoop dead center in my face, the last shred of punk sneer I hadn't retired yet. I didn't think twice about it. But after the event, one of Schaefer's bodyguards pulled me aside. "The Governor really likes you," he said, "but if you want to keep working for him, ditch the nose thing." That was it. No threats, no lecture. Just a reminder that Baltimore politics wasn't ready for a pierced-up photographer in the governor's entourage. I slipped the ring out and kept my mouth shut. Work was work.

Payment came only after I handed over the prints and the negatives. Every roll of film, every strip, surrendered into the machine. At the time, I didn't think about it. I was just happy to pocket the check. But now I wish I still had them --- not the staged smiles, but the backdrop, the frozen moments of Baltimore in the late '90s, a little time capsule that got swallowed by the political archive.

Schaefer himself had a soft spot for me once he found out who my grandfather was. Peter P. Belz Sr, "Perry", had been a legend in Hampden, founder and President of the Cresmont Social Club for over fifty years, a rowhouse-based fraternity of neighborhood power and beer taps. When Schaefer heard I was Perry's grandson, something shifted. Suddenly I wasn't just another hired shooter. I was part of the city's lineage, a link in the Hampden chain. He smiled wider when he shook my hand after that.

The money wasn't life-changing, but it plugged holes. When Thredhed had a slow week, or the sub-leasers were late with rent, those checks kept the lights on. One day I'd be photographing a governor kissing babies, the next I'd be booking piercing appointments or selling vintage fishnet stockings to Baltimores scenesters.

It was the duality of my life then --- vintage clothes upstairs, punk chaos downstairs, and every once in a while, a seat at the political table, camera in hand, capturing the polished face of power before hustling back to Hampden to make rent.

## Job #40: Freelance Stage Crew – Age 33 – 1997

Another side hustle that kept me alive in those years was stage crew work in Baltimore and DC. I wasn't running soundboards or designing lights. My niche was steel climbing --- the grunt labor of turning a bare field or hollow arena into a cathedral of scaffolding, cables, and lights. You showed up to empty space and, a few days later, you were looking up at a living skeleton of towers, trusses, and steel grids big enough to swallow a city block.

The work ran in three acts: build, run, tear down. We'd be there days before the first note was played, sweating and swearing as we bolted steel into shape. During the show, you had the run of the place. And when the crowd staggered out into the night, we climbed right back up to strip it all apart again. By the time the sun came up, the music was gone, and the field or stadium was empty, like it had all been a hallucination.

The perks, though, were undeniable. All-access badges meant you didn't buy a ticket --- you were the ticket. I leaned on barricades ten feet from Beck, perched on lighting towers while The Prodigy detonated basslines into the ground, and stood side-stage as Blondie came back from the dead, cool as they'd ever been. The veteran guys didn't care --- they smoked through sets, rolling their eyes at the noise. But this was a side gig for me, and I was there not only for a few extra bucks, but for the magic.

Breaks were their own strange world. We strung hammocks beneath stages, swaying like bats while 80,000 people stomped the ground all around us. The bass thudded through our ribs, a second heartbeat, while we dozed in the shadows. And then there was "shopping" --- the unspoken ritual of digging through jackets, backpacks, and purses tossed aside at the barricade and funneled under the stage. Lost-and-found in name only, treasure hunt in reality. Nobody said much about it. If we didn't pick through, it all ended up in the dumpster.

Safety was more suggestion than rule. OSHA existed, but it felt like folklore. I climbed fifty feet up in Doc Martens and a thin climbing belt, no helmet, no proper harness. My chalk bag didn't hold chalk --- it held weed, a one-hitter, a lighter, maybe a stubby cigar if I was feeling fancy. High-altitude survival kit, Baltimore-style. Every tool had to be tied off. A dropped wrench wasn't just clumsy, it was lethal. You never forgot how far gravity could carry something --- or someone.

The HFStival was the crown jewel. WHFS, the alternative radio beast of the time, threw this annual monster, and every band that mattered rolled through. From my perch in the steel, I watched a generation roar itself hoarse. Mud, sweat, bare chests painted in neon, crowd-surfers carried like corpses over waves of arms. Down below it looked like chaos. From up high, it looked choreographed, an organism moving as one.

For me, those gigs weren't just a paycheck. They were a reminder that work could be dangerous, dirty, and exhausting --- and still deliver something close to transcendence. One day you were bolting scaffolding with blistered hands, the next you were in the air, weed in your pocket, watching eighty thousand people lose their minds to music you didn't pay a dime to hear.

## Job #41: Web Page Designer – Age 33 – 1997

Web design in the late '90s wasn't the slick, templated world it is now. Back then, the internet still felt like a rumor with a busy signal. Every page was built the hard way --- pixel by pixel, code by code, trial by embarrassing error. My buddy John handled the back-end sorcery, writing lines of HTML that looked like Sanskrit to me. My role was the graphics and the hustle. I sold the clients, mocked up the visuals, and tried to convince small businesses that a website meant something in a world where most people still thought "going online" meant checking their answering machine.

We called the company **Spider Web**, which sounded edgy enough for the time, even if our "empire" fit on a single desk in the back office room at Thredhed. I had no training in design software, just sheer stubbornness and a Power Mac 7200. That machine was my workhorse, wheezing under the weight of Photoshop experiments while I clicked through menus like a lab rat pressing levers, trying to figure out which button made things bend, stretch, or glow. There were no filters, no drag-and-drop widgets. If I wanted a logo to look metallic, I had to build the shine from scratch, pixel by pixel, like painting chrome with a magnifying glass.

Most of our clients were mom-and-pop shops looking for some futuristic credibility. They didn't know what a website actually did, but they liked the idea of being "on the internet." The sites we built were clunky, loading one slow horizontal strip at a time while your modem wheezed like an asthmatic. If you didn't pay for a second phone line, being online meant your mother-in-law couldn't call to complain and nobody could reach you until you logged off. Half the time, I suspected the only people who ever saw our sites were the owners themselves, proudly showing their neighbors: "Look, we're on the World Wide Web!"

Spider Web was more ambition than business, but it had heart. Hilary, my girlfriend at the time and now my wife, had opened Nature's Web --- a health food store and juice bar right on the Avenue in Hampden. Together we dreamed up an online ordering and shipping system for her store. This was '97. Amazon was still selling mostly books. Grubhub didn't exist. The idea of ordering tinctures and extracts online was a punchline. Still, we imagined it. Nature's Web as a digital storefront, Hampden going high-tech.

That Power Mac 7200 was the link between all my worlds. It designed Jerkwater posters, ran Thredhed's experiments in digital flyers, and built the barebones websites for whatever hustles I was juggling. I'd sit there smoking up, toggling between layers, convinced that someday the world would catch up to what we were doing.

It was also the callback to one of the most important moments of my life. When Hilary first walked into my vintage shop looking for piercing jewelry, my pickup line was, "Want to be a model for my webpage?" She laughed and asked, "What's a webpage?" That line should've died on the floor, but somehow it worked. And now, years later, here we were actually building them together.

Most of the world still had no idea what a webpage even was, but Spider Web gave me another canvas. It was Hampden grit meeting digital frontier, thrift-store dust bleeding into pixelated neon. Nobody was paying us much, and half the time nobody was even watching, but it felt like peeking around the corner of the future --- and realizing we had already dragged a piece of our weird little world onto it.

### Job #42: Bar Manager – Age 34 – 1998

By then, I was burned out on hustles that didn't pay and bands that fizzled before they caught fire. Jerkwater had run its course. Thredhed was gone, sold off to Scott for pocket lint and goodwill. Hampden itself was starting to stir, but it wasn't yet the Instagram version of "quirky charm" it would eventually become. Back then it was still patchy --- one block alive with fresh energy, the next sagging with shuttered windows. I needed something steadier than a vintage shop, steadier than chasing gigs, steadier than waking up and wondering if the rent could actually get paid that month.

**Henninger's Tavern** gave me that.

Tucked on Fleet Street in Fells Point, it wasn't trying to be hip or reinvent the wheel. It already was something --- a neighborhood bar that felt like it had been sitting there for a hundred years, cluttered with knickknacks, walls layered with framed photographs, every inch of space heavy with story. You could come in three nights a week, sit at the same stool, and still notice something new hanging over the bar.

The place was run by Kenny and Jane, a husband-and-wife duo who knew how to balance art and chaos. Jane ruled the kitchen, and she didn't just feed people --- she made them rethink what bar food could be. Her fried oysters with Pernod sauce stopped me in my tracks. Salty, rich, licorice bite cutting through the brine --- it was the kind of dish that made you pause mid-sentence and nod like someone had just whispered a secret in your ear.

Kenny handled the front with a collector's soul. His record collection was legendary, thousands of albums spanning old jazz and forgotten R&B. He curated nights like a DJ before DJs had laptops --- slipping into a little side room, pulling out a record, cueing it up, and letting the needle drop. The soundtrack was never background; it was the bar's bloodstream. Without Kenny's vinyl obsession, Henninger's would have been just another joint with good oysters. With it, the place pulsed with mood.

When I came in as Bar Manager, I found ways to bend the edges. One of my favorite tricks was reimagining the menu covers. I'd photograph our regulars, then splice their faces into old historical portraits --- sepia Civil War generals, Washington crossing the Delaware, sometimes old tintype-style oddities. Early Photoshop, clunky and slow, but powerful enough to turn drunks into icons. The covers became a running joke, and soon the regulars weren't just asking what the soup of the day was --- they were asking when they'd get their shot at menu immortality.

The nights had rhythm. Regulars holding down their spots at the bar, first-timers drifting in from outside the neighborhood, couples settling into the corner tables. Fells Point was still rough then, cobblestones slick with beer spills and the echoes of old dockworker ghosts, but Henninger's carried its own warmth. It wasn't just drinks and food --- it was memory layered over memory, music drifting through the ghost of a thousand conversations.

For me, it was the reset I needed. Steady income, creative sparks, a chance to exhale after years of chasing every side hustle I could get my hands on. It wasn't glamorous, but it didn't need to be. It was work with edges worn smooth, a tavern where every night felt like it was in on the joke. And for a while, that was enough.

## Job #43: Loan Officer – Age 35 – 1999

Eric and his wife were fixtures at Henninger's. Almost nightly they'd slide onto their usual stools, order their drinks, and talk about the day. They weren't loud, they weren't dramatic, but they were consistent --- the kind of regulars that form the backbone of a bar. Over time, Eric started pitching me on his world. He owned a mortgage company called **Charm City Mortgage**, and one night, somewhere between his second and third drink, he leaned in and said, "You should come work for me. You'll make a lot more money than you're making here."

I laughed it off at first. I was the guy running a bar, Photoshopping regulars into Civil War portraits, still living in a world where creativity was currency. Finance wasn't just foreign to me; it was the enemy --- the gray cubicle universe I had avoided my entire working life. But I was engaged, thinking about marriage, kids, the next step. Money suddenly had a weight it never had before. When he promised to train me and get me up to speed fast, I heard more than a job offer. I heard security.

Walking into Charm City Mortgage was like landing on another planet. Henninger's had been a shrine to sound and taste --- jazz records spinning, Pernod sauce simmering in the kitchen, the walls packed with a lifetime of artifacts. Charm City had nothing but beige walls, clunky phones, and metal file cabinets. Instead of jazz and oysters, there were ringing phones, bad coffee, and the soft stink of paper and toner.

Training wasn't really training. It was osmosis. You sat next to a guy, listened to him work a lead, and then tried to do it yourself. There was no salary, no safety net. You hunted your own business, convinced strangers to refinance, consolidate debt, or cash out equity, and if the deal closed, you got paid. If it didn't, you starved. The place had the energy of a boiler room, except dressed up in khakis and polos.

The products we sold were perfectly legal but ethically slippery. "No doc" loans, "lite doc" loans --- paperwork that let people sign away their futures without much scrutiny. A homeowner might walk in looking to pull out a few thousand for a new deck, and by the time the ink dried, I was making more in commission than they were actually taking home. Everyone smiled, the deal got filed, the company made its money, and no one said out loud what we all knew --- the math didn't favor the homeowner.

Some months it felt like I had struck gold. A handful of deals closed back-to-back and suddenly I was holding checks bigger than anything I'd ever made in kitchens, bars, or warehouses. Then came the droughts. Leads dried up, calls went unanswered, deals fell apart in underwriting. The phone would sit silent on my desk, and the knot in my stomach would tighten by the day. Commission life wasn't feast and famine --- it was feast and starvation.

What I did learn was how credit really works, how banks package debt, how people dig themselves into holes they can't climb out of. It was like getting a crash course in the underbelly of the American Dream. And it forced me to face something about myself. I could do the job. I could sell the loans, chase the deals, cash the checks. But at the end of the day, I couldn't shake the feeling that I was making money off other people's chains.

For a guy who had once made bar menus by cutting and pasting regulars into historical portraits, that realization hit hard. Creativity made me feel alive. Debt made me feel complicit. And that was the difference that would never balance out.

**Job #44: Insurance Agent – Age 37 – 2001**

After limping through the mortgage world, I decided to level up. A family member nudged me toward insurance, swearing it was the respectable path. Forget the Wild West of loans, they said --- this was a real profession, regulated, stable, the kind of career you could put on a business card without smirking. So I landed at **John Hancock Financial Services**, a place where credibility dripped from the mahogany furniture and the ties were knotted with precision.

The indoctrination started fast. Licensing exams, endless study sessions, compliance manuals thicker than Bibles. By the time I was done, I had the licenses and the "credibility" to sell long-term care insurance, variable annuities, and mutual funds. On paper, I was a financial professional. In reality, I was a glorified telemarketer in a suit.

The daily grind was 300 cold calls. Three. Hundred. Every day. A headset digging into my ear, a script in front of me, a spreadsheet of strangers' numbers, and a quota that never eased up. You dial, you pitch, you get hung up on. You dial again. A rhythm set to rejection. Maybe one in a hundred calls got past "Hello." Most ended in slammed receivers or muttered curses. You could hear the fatigue in the whole room --- twenty voices, all talking over each other, trying to sound chipper while slowly dying inside.

The office itself looked polished but felt hollow. Cubicles in tight rows, the faint buzz of fluorescent lights, motivational posters framed on the walls like cheap jokes. "Success is a journey," one read. The only journey most of us wanted was the one out the door at 5:01. But nobody said that out loud. We wore the suits, we carried the briefcases, we played the roles.

And that was the part I weirdly excelled at --- the role. Years earlier, I'd been in a college improv group. Insurance felt like one long improv sketch. Put on the costume, step into character, hit your marks. Behind the mask, I was the same tattooed, pierced, music-obsessed guy I'd always been, but in that office I was "Belz, Financial Services Professional." I even ran a prank to keep my sanity: threading a paperclip through my septum piercing when no one was looking, flashing it to the kid in the next cubicle, who'd try to prove it to others. By the time he dragged anyone over, the clip was gone, leaving him sputtering. It was stupid, juvenile, but it reminded me that I still had a pulse.

What I couldn't joke away was the sales culture. Every success was measured in numbers --- policies written, premiums locked, commissions earned. I made the National Leaderboard one quarter after rolling a few 401(k)'s into annuities, and for a couple months I was an office darling. But that didn't last long. There were no regular paychecks, just commission. That meant feast or famine. Land a few big annuities? You were king for the month. Go cold for two weeks? You were broke. It made for a manic cycle of confidence and despair. We all knew it, even if we wore our ties straight and smiled like we had the market cornered.

Long-term care insurance was the foot in the door. The "easy" sell. People were terrified of nursing homes, of losing everything to medical bills. Once you had them talking, you could pivot: roll their 401(k) into a variable annuity, pitch them on mutual funds, slide them into a whole "financial plan." That was the real bread and butter. That's where the big commissions hid. It wasn't about protecting families. It was about moving product, keeping the machine fed.

The longer I sat at that desk, the more I saw the cracks. The seniors we pitched long-term care to often didn't have the means to pay the premiums for long. The annuities we pushed weren't always in the clients' best interest. The language was always technically correct --- disclosures, prospectuses, compliance boxes checked --- but it was theater. A show. Just like the "grip and grin" shots I'd taken for Governor Schaefer a few years earlier, only this time I was the one grinning, gripping hands with clients, pretending the script was sincere.

I did learn the mechanics of finance --- credit scores, asset allocation, the alphabet soup of licenses and products. I learned how to talk money in a room full of conservative professionals without them ever guessing about the tattoos under my sleeves or the music I cranked in the car on the way home. But every lesson came with an aftertaste. Respectability had a price, and the longer I wore the role, the more it felt like the costume was swallowing me whole.

**Job #45: Actor – Age 37 – 2001**

Most people walk into acting through auditions, headshots, résumés. I walked in through Hampden, like I did with half the weird shit in my life. **Truck Stop Productions** had an office right off the Avenue. One of their guys knew me from around the neighborhood and remembered I'd done improv back at Towson. That was apparently enough to get me cast in a pizza commercial.

Not just any pizza commercial. A Ledo's Pizza commercial shot in the basement of an abandoned psychiatric hospital. Imagine the smell of damp plaster, peeling lead paint curling off the walls, fluorescent lights flickering just enough to make you feel like you were about to be wheeled into electroshock. Then drop a bunch of grown adults into costumes shaped like cardboard pizza-box corners. That was the set.

The premise was insane, literally. A group therapy session for incomplete pizza boxes, each of them moaning about how empty our lives felt. They were lopsided, unsatisfied, forever missing something. My role? The counselor. The straight man in a room full of cardboard casualties. The gag was simple enough: Ledo's made square pizzas, which meant their boxes were complete. No therapy needed. Comedy by geometry.

There wasn't much of a script at first. The producers gave us the setup and then told us to riff. We leaned into the absurdity, trying to one-up each other's lines. My job was to keep the circus from spinning off its axis, playing it deadpan, feeding them prompts like a real shrink would. The crew was cracking up behind the cameras. Eventually, they stitched together the best lines into a loose framework and declared it done.

And then it aired. Constantly. Baltimore got saturated with my pizza-box therapy face. I couldn't walk into a bar without someone squinting at me and saying, "Wait... were you in that commercial?" My fifteen minutes of fame weren't glamorous. They were square. Ledo's square.

The peak came when the two halves of my life smashed together. I was in a client's living room, tie knotted, briefcase open, flipping through John Hancock long-term care brochures. The TV was murmuring in the background when suddenly, there I was, onscreen in a pizza-box group session. The client froze, pointed at the screen, then back at me. "Hey! That's you!" he shouted. Then he bellowed upstairs: "Honey, the insurance man is on TV dressed up as a pizza box!"

I wanted to sink through the floor, but he loved it. Thought it was hysterical. The deal closed. Ledo's sold pizza, Hancock sold insurance, and I got paid in both worlds.

For a few months, I was Baltimore's most recognizable fake therapist for incomplete cardboard. Not a résumé booster, not a career, just one more strange chapter — the day job in pinstripes, the side hustle in corrugated comedy. And you can still see that commercial on YouTube if you search: Ledo's Pizza Best Commercial Ever

**Job #46: Settlement Officer – Age 39 – 2003**

By the time I left John Hancock, I was done with the constant cold calls, the starched shirts, the forced optimism about annuities and long-term care. Insurance felt like a straitjacket. **Omni Land Settlement**, on the other hand, promised something else: real people, real work, a paycheck without the theater of dialing 300 strangers a day. I already knew their crew from my loan officer days, so the jump wasn't so much a leap as sliding into a new chair at a table I'd already been sitting at.

The job itself was a grind, but a strange kind of grind. I was a settlement officer --- half notary, half road warrior, part therapist, part human paperclip. Refinances, purchases, closings stacked five or six deep in a day, spread across four or five states. Pennsylvania, Delaware, Maryland, Virginia, D.C. --- all fair game. To do it, I had to become a notary in every single one. My briefcase looked like the passport control station at a border nobody wanted to cross.

This was pre-GPS, the dark ages before phones chirped directions into your ear. My navigation arsenal was a mix of worn-out Rand McNally road atlases, hand-scribbled directions from clients who thought "turn at the old red barn" counted as a landmark, and eventually the miracle of MapQuest. Printing out ten sets of turn-by-turns every morning felt futuristic at the time, even if each page took forever to crawl out of a sputtering inkjet. The stack of papers in the passenger seat looked like a novel, and good luck if you missed an exit and had to improvise mid-route.

Most closing settlements were bland enough --- kitchen tables, suburban basements, conference rooms in half-empty office parks. But every now and then the script went sideways.

Southern Maryland. Remote property, driveway gravel crunching under my tires. The garage door stood wide open, fluorescent light buzzing inside. I knocked at the front door, got nothing. Knocked again, louder. That's when he appeared --- a man in his fifties, hands and forearms soaked in blood, shirt streaked red like he'd crawled out of a horror film.

Every survival instinct in me screamed. Three exits flashed in my head: grab a landscaping rock and swing, sprint for the car and pray the engine turned over, or go down swinging with my notary stamp as a weapon. My pulse was hammering before he even opened his mouth.

"Oh, sorry," he said casually, like he'd just tracked mud onto the carpet. "Didn't hear you pull up. I'm out back skinning rabbits."

And just like that, the tension deflated. Still, shaking the man's hand ten minutes later while closing his refinance paperwork, I couldn't stop staring at the faint brown stains around his cuticles. There are polite excuses, and then there's "Sorry I'm dripping rabbit blood on your mortgage docs."

Then there was Route 50. Tight on-ramp toward D.C., me easing my way in, radio low, mind already halfway at the next appointment. Out of nowhere, an old pickup truck came flying backwards up the ramp, pedal mashed to the floor, driver drunk or insane. He hit me head-on before I had time to swear. My little sedan folded like a soda can, antifreeze spraying into the side of the highway, steam hissing up in the afternoon air.

His truck barely had a dent. He climbed out, swaying, slurring something about how his truck was fine so he was leaving. Just like that. If another driver hadn't pulled over and blocked him, he would've been gone. Even then, the guy floored it, nearly mowing the good Samaritan down. He cried, "He tried to kill me!" I replied, "Yeah he did!" The witness jumped back in his own truck and gave chase, disappearing in a cloud of dust like something out of a bad cop show.

I sat there on the shoulder, alone with my wreckage, wondering if I'd just imagined the whole thing. Thirty minutes later the cops rolled up. Before I could open my mouth, the officer cut me off. "We got him." Turns out the chase ended with the drunk flipping his truck and bailing on foot. He took off into the woods along the highway, but didn't get far.

It even made the local news. High-speed chase on Route 50, truck on its roof, drunk in cuffs. I was mentioned as -- - Baltimore County Man. For a minute I thought I was going to be dragged into court, maybe testify, but months later I heard the charges were dropped. Why, I'll never know. Money, connections, or just the randomness of the justice system.

That was Omni in a nutshell. You could spend the morning notarizing papers for a sweet couple in matching sweaters, the afternoon dodging drunk drivers, and the evening standing in the doorway of a garage with blood dripping onto the concrete. Every "t" crossed, every "i" dotted, and still chaos always found a way in.

### Job #47 – Children's Entertainer – Age 39 – 2003

By 2003, my workdays were already kid-saturated. Two young children at home meant diapers, playground mulch in my shoes, and a steady barrage of children's music weaponized to drill itself into adult skulls. The Wiggles, Laurie Berkner, Dan Zanes --- they were less musicians and more psychological operatives, planting earworms so durable they survived grocery lines, gas pumps, even my dreams. The kids would hear "Fruit Salad, Yummy Yummy," dance around the living room for three minutes, and then move on. I'd still be whistling the damn thing six hours later, wondering if this was how people went insane.

The itch to make music again hit me at the same time my tolerance for these sing-song mantras bottomed out. My brother Joe had a hard drive full of instrumental songs, unfinished ideas he hadn't touched. I started listening to them with Raffi and Sesame Street still rattling around in my head, and suddenly those instrumental tracks sounded like a blueprint. What if we built something for kids, but made it ours?

That was the spark for **The Bigtops**.

We went circus. Full tilt. I became Barnaby Bigtop, ringmaster, dressed in a rainbow tuxedo with tails that looked like Willy Wonka had been mugged by Ringling Brothers. Melissa, my friend and co-vocalist, became Oopsy Daisy, shimmering in a silver sequin get-up that caught every stray beam of light like a disco ball. Carol, a movement specialist, rounded it out as Betty Ballerina. She never sang or spoke --- just floated, twirled, and pantomimed across the stage like a silent film star smuggled into a children's party.

The first time we suited up, I realized we'd basically turned ourselves into human fever dreams; polyester sweat lodges masquerading as costumes. At festivals, you could smell us before you saw us. But the kids didn't care. They shrieked, clapped, jumped in place like our sweaty misery was the greatest show on earth.

We recorded an album --- The Big Hello --- kid-friendly songs layered over Joe's old tracks that I had written some lyrics for, a mix of circus-barker vocals from me and powerhouse belting from Melissa. Somehow, decades later, it's still floating around on Spotify. Melissa kept performing long after as Ultra Sharlat, but for a while, she was my co-conspirator in turning circus chaos into family entertainment.

The gigs were surreal: backyard birthday parties where our "stage" was a patch of grass between a swing set and a grill, community festivals where the funnel cake lines were longer than our audience. The kids didn't care about the details --- to them, Barnaby was Barnaby, Oopsy was Oopsy, Betty was Betty. They screamed, sang, and collapsed into piles of giggles no matter what we did.

The real test came two days before one of our bigger shows. Mid-rehearsal, I jumped the wrong way, heard the crack, and realized I'd broken a bone in my foot. The sensible move would've been to cancel. Instead, I showed up with a cast, stiff-legged and hobbling, compensating with cartoonish arm swings and exaggerated gestures. I leaned into the ringmaster persona harder than ever, bellowing "Step right up, come on inside…!" in my best vaudeville boom. The kids went wild, Melissa carried the vocals, Carol twirled, and the parents nodded, impressed we'd kept the show rolling. Painkillers and adrenaline did the rest.

The Bigtops never became the next Wiggles. We didn't tour, didn't sign contracts, didn't chase Nickelodeon or PBS. What we did have was a handful of shows, one album, and a string of memories that stitched my love of music directly into my role as a father. For once, I wasn't just in the audience of my kids' childhood soundtrack --- I was part of the band.

Looking back, it was ridiculous, exhausting, and completely worth it. For a few years, Barnaby Bigtop wasn't just a character. He was my way of stepping into my kids' world, sequins, sweat, broken foot and all.

### Job #48 – Musician – Age 41 – 2005

After the polyester circus tent of The Bigtops, I needed volume again. Children's music had been fun, surreal even, but I wasn't built to spend the rest of my life crooning about umbrellas and playdough. Somewhere under the Barnaby Bigtop tuxedo, I was still the guy who wanted to rattle walls with guitars and drums. Hilary must have felt it too, because one birthday she handed me a brand-new electric guitar.

It was like she had slipped me a hall pass back to my own noise. I didn't know a G chord from an F, didn't care. I taught myself enough to bash out riffs, string words together, and write songs that didn't need polish. Technique was optional. Conviction was mandatory.

That was the birth of **Shineola**.

I was living in Pennsylvania at the time, but the band's gravity pulled me back to Baltimore every week. Practices were at Sam's place, gear crammed into his studio, walls sweating with volume. The lineup was solid: Joe on lead guitar, Tim on bass, Sam on drums, me handling rhythm and vocals. I wrote the songs, half-shouted them into the mic, and we leaned into the sound --- loud, driving, straight-ahead rock with a streak of optimism that somehow cut through the distortion.

We weren't kids anymore. Most of the bands we played with were still carding at the door, barely old enough to order a beer, but we liked it that way. Instead of feeling out of place, we leaned into it. We had scars, jobs, kids, divorces, and still we were making noise. We carried ourselves with a swagger that came from having lived entire lives before showing up to plug into Marshall stacks. We weren't chasing the dream. We were already awake, and that made us dangerous in our own small way.

Our first demo, Cream of the Slop, was recorded in Joe's basement studio in his house in Hampden. Later we booked real studio time, tracked a handful of songs, but they never saw daylight. Still, hearing those mixes through real monitors, crisp and punishing, was a thrill all its own.

For a little over a year, Shineola had juice. We packed local rooms, pulled respectable crowds, and left behind enough of a trace to prove we weren't just weekend warriors. My nephew Nick made a video of us at the Ottobar, hammering through our song "Blanket". That video footage still sits on YouTube, fossilized evidence that in my forties --- with kids, bills, and all the gravity of adulthood pressing down --- I could still strap on a guitar, howl into a microphone, and feel the crowd surge back at me.

We didn't break out. No record deals, no tours, no magazine spreads. But that wasn't the point. Shineola was proof that noise still lived in me, proof that fatherhood and mortgages didn't erase the need to get loud. For a year or so, I got to step back into the glare of stage lights, chest vibrating with the force of amps, sweat dripping, the room moving with us.

Shineola didn't last, but it didn't have to. It was fuel, catharsis, a reminder that the circus wasn't my last act. The noise was still mine.


**Job #49 – Café Owner – Age 43 – 2007**

By 2007, Hilary and I had packed up the kids and moved north to Pennsylvania so they could attend the Waldorf School. I was still grinding away at settlement work, but the pull of food had been gnawing at me for years. When the chance came to buy a little pizza joint in Marietta with Hilary's father, we jumped. We jazzed it up, renamed it the **New Day Café,** and decided to do things our way: breakfast, lunch, pizzas, and whenever possible, organic and local. We weren't just slinging slices. We wanted to drag a sleepy river town into the present.

Marietta wasn't exactly crying out for panini's and free-range organic eggs. Population maybe 2,000, a handful of bars hanging on by their fingernails, the kind of place where the sidewalks rolled up after dark. But beneath the closed-up storefronts, the town carried its own folklore. Old-timers would tell you about the days when it was a logging hub, a stopover for men floating timber down the Susquehanna. Back then Marietta was a boomtown of brothels and saloons --- fights, drinking, sex, and trouble on every corner. A place where you either held your own or went under. By the time we showed up, the ghosts of that chaos still lingered in the cracked brick and faded paint, but the action was long gone. We were planting an organic café in the middle of a town that barely had a grocery store.

The ovens became my church. Every morning I showed up before dawn, unlocking the door to that cold, empty room. The ritual started with dough. High-gluten flour, water, salt, yeast --- that was the alchemy. The dough was alive, shifting with the weather, the humidity, my own mood. Some mornings it was cooperative, elastic, ready to be shaped. Others it fought back, tight and stubborn, daring me to force it into something edible. Cooking was in my bones, and dough had a way of reminding me that no matter what else was happening, my hands could still create something worth putting on a plate.

But romance doesn't pay the bills. For the first nine months I lived in the café --- 80-hour weeks, perspiration soaked into my clothes, barely seeing my kids except when they visited the shop. We scraped by, inching toward break-even, praying each month's books didn't sink us. There were sparks of joy, though. A pair of regulars once came in panicked, telling us their wedding officiant had bailed two weeks before the big day. I pulled out my laptop, got ordained online in about ten minutes, and told them I'd marry them myself. Two weeks later I was standing on the banks of the Susquehanna River, dressed like a half-baked preacher, binding two people together because they trusted the pizza guy to do it. That's the kind of town Marietta was --- small enough that your local café owner could end up the one making your marriage official.

And then 2008 rolled in like a sledgehammer. The recession didn't just rattle Wall Street; it gutted the price of every ingredient we touched. A 50-pound bag of flour that cost $11.75 shot up to seventy-two bucks almost overnight. Seventy-two dollars for flour. Margins disappeared. Customers started counting pennies. We were working ourselves into the ground, bleeding cash, and there was no bailout waiting for us. Banks got saved. Cafés like ours didn't.

Eventually I looked around --- at the ovens, the flour, the empty dining room on a Tuesday afternoon --- and realized I was out. I had no money, no time left for my kids, and no interest in grinding myself into the ground for a business that wasn't going to make it through the storm. We locked the doors. Another casualty of a crash caused by people in suits who never set foot in places like Marietta.

The café didn't last, but it burned itself into me. I rediscovered my love for cooking, my respect for dough, and my appetite for early mornings in a kitchen filled with heat and possibility. For a short while, we dropped a flare of energy into a town that had once been all grit and whiskey. Even if New Day couldn't survive, it proved something to me: passion can fuel a place, but passion alone doesn't pay the flour bill when it jumps sixfold overnight.

### Job #50 – Musician – Age 43 – 2007

Shineola had burned out, but the itch didn't. You don't just hang up the noise when it's in your bones. I was running the New Day Café, flipping pizzas and frying eggs in a sleepy river town, but after the ovens cooled and the chairs were stacked, I needed something louder, nastier.

So I started a band with Dylan, one of my waiters, and Brad, a regular at the café who lived in the neighborhood. We called it **Mumbly Peg**, after the knife game kids used to play in dirt lots, flinging blades at their own shoes for bragging rights. It fit. Our music was stripped to the bone --- three pieces, no polish, no mercy. Me, as the songwriter on guitar and vocals, Dylan on bass, Brad on drums. Old-school hardcore punk, played like it was supposed to hurt.

I never thought of myself as a "singer." My voice wasn't melodic; it was a bark, a sneer, a rusted crowbar swung at the mic. The lyrics weren't sermons. They were barbed-wire mantras, shouted until your throat shredded. The guitar was a blunt weapon, not a delicate instrument. Mumbly Peg wasn't about finesse. It was about speed, volume, and catharsis.

Rehearsals were held in the café itself. Once a week, after the last customer wandered out and the coffee machine cooled, we pushed the tables to the walls, cranked the amps, and shook the building like we were exorcising ghosts. The smell of coffee and grease still hung in the air, mixing with sweat and distortion until the whole place felt like a contradiction --- breakfast joint by day, punk venue by night. The tenant upstairs endured it all in exchange for reduced rent. A fair deal.

Eventually, we decided to record. That meant a trip to The Shanty, a ramshackle outbuilding behind Dylan's friend Elias's place in Marietta. The Shanty was part clubhouse, part squat, part smoke-filled den where the local kids burned off their boredom. It was legendary in its own way: broken furniture, walls tagged with stickers, the air permanently fogged with pot smoke and cheap beer. Nobody asked whose beer was whose --- by the end of the night it all blended into the same warm backwash anyway.

Elias had cobbled together a modest recording setup in the corner, as he had a background in recording; I think he went to school for it. We hammered out our EP, Girl Song, in one manic burst. A day, maybe two. No overdubs, no polish, no "fix it in the mix." Just raw takes, amps buzzing, mistakes left in because they felt honest. The tracks were jagged, imperfect, loud as hell --- exactly what we were.

That little EP survived. Somehow, Girl Song still floats around online years later on all the streaming services, streaming alongside polished records we never would've dreamed of sharing a shelf with. Proof that for a short time, three guys in a café-turned-practice-space managed to bottle lightning.

Mumbly Peg didn't last long. Punk bands rarely do. But while it burned, it was alive --- coffee in the morning, distortion at night, the grind of café survival feeding the fury of three chords slammed into any place that would have us.. No fame, no fortune. Just noise, sweat, and a defiant middle finger carved into the quiet of small-town Pennsylvania.

### Job #51 – Deli Counter Man – Age 44 – 2008

After the café went under, I landed at **Edmart Deli** in Reisterstown, MD, a kosher Jewish institution that had been feeding Baltimore for half a century. Calling it a "deli" felt reductive. It wasn't just a place to grab a sandwich --- it was a temple where pastrami had the same spiritual heft as scripture, where arguments about schmaltz could spiral into full-blown theology.

I got in through my father-in-law, who was friendly with the owner, Shelley. He was toying with the idea of investing and wanted me to "size things up." Translation: go work behind the counter and report back if this circus was worth sinking money into. Spoiler: it wasn't.

Shelley had just inherited the place after her father --- the patriarch who ran it for over fifty years --- died. She wore the crown because it had been passed down, not because she'd been trained to run the kingdom. Which meant every day was a balancing act: tradition pulling one way, chaos tugging the other.

The shop itself was small, divided by an invisible line sharper than any blade in the kitchen: meat case on one side, dairy case on the other. Separate slicers, separate cutting boards, separate knives, separate logic. Cross that line with the wrong product, and you might as well have declared war. Want corned beef and Swiss? Fine, we'd sell them both — but bagged separately. The sin was yours to commit at home or in the car, not under our roof. Every week a rabbi came by to bless the shop, and somehow the blessing always ended with him hauling away a doggie bag stuffed with smoked fish and kugel. Holiness with a side of chopped liver.

The food was glorious. Brisket so tender it surrendered at the touch of a fork. Gefilte fish that looked like it belonged in a natural history exhibit but still tasted like comfort to the people who grew up with it. Mountains of smoked salmon, sable, whitefish, herring in cream — the whole place smelled like the North Atlantic had come ashore on Reisterstown Road. My favorite, though, was the brisket knishes. We made them from scraps, folding fatty shreds of slow-cooked brisket into dough and baking them into golden pockets that stuck to your ribs in the best way. They ruined me. To this day, living in Pennsylvania, I can't find a decent knish, let alone one stuffed with brisket trimmings.

Of course, I was the oddball. The tattooed goy behind the counter. To the old-timers, I looked like a punk rock roadie who'd wandered in after a show, and they squinted at me like I might accidentally baptize the nova. What saved me was my knife work. Hand-slicing lox so thin you could read the City Paper through it became my redemption arc. Precision buys you respect. Within weeks, people were asking for me by name. In the deli world, respect is measured in millimeters.

Behind the counter, though, it was pure madness. Shelley ruled with the paranoia of a monarch in exile, convinced no one else could grasp the delicate geopolitics of smoked fish and kugel inventory. Orders got barked, countermen grumbled, and the whole operation somehow stumbled forward, day after day, powered by brisket, bagels, and sheer inertia.

After six months, I delivered the verdict to my father-in-law: if you want to lose money, just drive to Atlantic City and put it all on black. It'll be quicker and less stressful. Then I hung up the apron and walked away, clothes forever carrying the perfume of smoked whitefish. There are worse fates, sure. But once you've lived inside a kosher deli's chaos, you don't forget it — the smell lingers longer than the paycheck.

## Job #52 – Crew Work – Age 44 – 2008

During this stretch I was also hustling side gigs with my friend Tim, the old Shineola bass player. He had started a company called **Charm City Crew Works** and would call me in when he really needed extra hands, or I would call him if I wanted to score a cool show. Most of it was stage grunt work: loading trucks, hauling amps, wrangling gear off buses. Hard labor for short money, but I liked the atmosphere. Backstage was always a mix of sweat, smoke, and all-access passes. Good weed floated around, and even if the "talent" usually treated you like scenery, there were moments that made it worth it.

One of those moments came at a Ministry show at Club Sonar. The venue was the perfect industrial cave for them, cavernous, gritty, and humming with the kind of dangerous energy their music always seemed to conjure. As I stood side-stage watching the gear get finalized, it hit me that the last time I had seen Ministry live was back in 1989 at Shriver Hall on the Johns Hopkins campus.

That first show was unforgettable. Ministry was joined onstage by some of the members of Skinny Puppy, and they turned the place into a madhouse. They were all over the stage, crawling over monitors, bodies flying everywhere, lights strobing like a seizure waiting to happen. It felt less like a concert and more like a ritual, something primal and unhinged, and I walked out of there half-deaf, half-possessed, convinced I had just seen something otherworldly.

Now, almost twenty years later, I wasn't in the crowd. I wasn't a wide-eyed kid clutching my ticket stub. I was crew, wearing a laminate around my neck, making sure amps got moved, cables stayed coiled, and production didn't collapse. The Revolting Cocks, Jourgenson's other band, were opening that night. Right before they went on, Jourgenson himself walked up to me, handed me a t-shirt, and said, "Hey man, this is for you. Thanks for all your hard work." A small gesture, but pure class in rock and roll currency.

The shirt was black, with a Revolting Cocks logo on one sleeve, a Ministry logo on the other, and across the chest: Mastabatour Local Crew. I still have it. Proof that I had come full circle, from a kid in the crowd watching Ministry and Skinny Puppy tear Baltimore to shreds, to part of the unseen army making it all happen at Sonar.

For the other crew guys around me, it was just another show, another load-in and load-out, another night of smoke and sweat. But for me, it was magic. A reminder that sometimes life loops back in ways you never expect --- one night you're in the audience losing your mind, the next you're backstage holding a piece of that world in your hands.

### Job #53 – Director of Food Services – Age 45 – 2009

Then **Kimberton Wholefoods** came knocking. Their HR manager, Lydia, had been a regular at my old café and pitched me hard: they wanted me to take over food service operations for a brand-new Lancaster store. At the same time, I'd been sketching out my own idea for a Jewish-style deli in Lancaster Central Market, hand-slicing nova, brisket knishes, the works. But I shelved it. Kimberton looked safer, steadier. The right move for a family man.

They hired me as "Director of Food Services" straight off. Lancaster was supposed to be my kingdom. But when I showed up, there was no store, just a whisper of one. Instead, they tossed me into a bare warehouse with nothing but empty floor space and told me to make it operational and act as the warehouse manager. So I did. I bolted racks together, mapped flow, got trucks moving in and out. I told myself it was a temporary detour --- Lancaster was the end game.

But months passed. No store. Then Terry, the owner, asked me to start commuting to the Kimberton location and whip their food service into shape. Kimberton was ninety minutes each way. I wanted no part of that grind. I pushed back. That's when they dangled a "company car."

It wasn't a car so much as a tetanus risk on four bad tires. Rust, rattles, dashboard held together with duct tape. But it ran, and running meant the impossible commute became barely possible. What was supposed to be short-term stretched into a year and a half of me in that rolling coffin, grinding up and down Pennsylvania turnpike for the promise of a store that still didn't exist.

At Kimberton, I killed off the sad little café that had been slinging quesadillas and breakfast sandwiches like it was still 1992. In its place, I built a real hot bar program, expanded grab-and-go across the chain, and installed costing systems to stop the bleeding. For all the dysfunction, I was proud of what I carved out of that mess.

But the grind broke me down. One night driving home, my body just gave out. My teeth started chattering, my hands locked around the steering wheel like claws, and I could barely steer. Somehow I limped back to the house, stumbled through the door, and collapsed. Hilary thought it was a heart attack. Ambulance, hospital, IVs. Diagnosis: diverticulitis, infection raging like a bonfire in my gut. It was Thanksgiving the next day and for the first time since we were married, we couldn't host it for our families. The in-laws picked up the slack. Thanksgiving dinner for my family was turkey and stuffing. For me, fluorescent Jell-O and the smell of antiseptic, as I was three days in the hospital.

I went back to work on Monday like nothing happened, stitched together with caffeine and stubbornness, but the truth was obvious: I was running on fumes, betting it all on Lancaster. Then Terry dropped the hammer. He'd been talking to consultants, and they convinced him to pull the plug. Lancaster was dead. The store I'd been promised, the one I'd built my whole pitch around, was gone. And with it went the clunker --- the only thing that had made the brutal commute tolerable.

That was it. Without Lancaster, without the car, without trust, there was nothing left. I kept showing up long enough to hand things off clean, but inside I was done. Betrayed, strung along, sold a dream that evaporated on someone else's bad advice.

On the way out, I found a spark. I'd been homebrewing on the side, chasing yeast, barley and hops like old friends. Hilary suggested I take it further. I signed up for an online course, studied obsessively, and became a Certified Cicerone Beer Server. Almost nobody knew what that was yet, but I didn't care. It lit me up. Beer styles, brewing history, the science behind fermentation --- it was like discovering a new language.

Kimberton had chewed me up and spit me out. But it shoved me sideways into something better, something alive. And for the first time in years, I felt like I was back at the starting line of something that mattered.

### Job #54 – Craft Beer Specialist – Age 47 – 2011

In 2011, "craft beer" was still a shaky phrase, not the cultural monolith it would later become. People were just learning to trade in the word "microbrew," and outside the beer nerd bubble, it was still alien territory. Most bar owners thought IPA was a typo. Regulars ordered Miller, or Yuengling, or the occasional Bud and if you suggested anything else, they'd look at you like you'd just pissed in their shot of whiskey.

That's when I landed at **Nevulis Beverages**. On paper, my new title --- "Craft Beer Specialist" --- sounded like I was about to lead the charge of some foamy, hop-fueled revolution. In reality, Nevulis was a circus without a tent. The family had run a respected retail beer store for years, and decided to try the wholesale distribution game. But when it came to distribution, they were amateurs playing dress-up.

There wasn't even a walk-in cooler. Kegs sat in rented offices with the air conditioner cranked, sweating and spoiling while the sales team --- eight of us --- fought over a single delivery truck. Orders got scribbled down, promised to accounts, then never showed. It wasn't a business. It was a brewery-themed farce, like watching Dumb and Dumber try to run a beverage company.

Still, I believed. I loved beer, loved the idea of dragging the country tavern crowd out of their Lite-beer haze and into something alive. Every time I cracked a bottle of Belgian dubbel or poured a pint of IPA for someone who'd never tasted one before, I felt like I was handing them a secret password. That belief carried me while the business around me crumbled.

Then came the money bomb. Ownership decided we'd all be moved from salary-plus-commission to straight commission, as if dangling survival by a thread would magically solve their logistics nightmare. My check went from predictable to roulette. I wasn't about to beg. Instead, I cut a deal with John, the owner: if I could land a major distributor to sub-distribute our portfolio, he'd reinstate my salary, and I would manage that distributor.

I picked my target: Ace Distributing out of York. They were old-school, serious, had some craft beers and a craft brand manager. I threw everything I had at them. The passion, the history, the conviction that craft wasn't a fad but a tidal shift. The funny part was that the brands we carried weren't even worth a second glance --- most of them don't exist today. But I could sell the story, and against all odds, Ace bought it.

That should have been the victory lap. Ace was credibility, coverage, stability. Exactly the lifeline Nevulis needed. We went out to a diner to celebrate, the kind of sad little place where the coffee tastes like burnt tires and the eggs are slick with grease. Over Formica and fluorescent lights, I brought up my salary.

John didn't even blink. "You're staying on commission," he said flatly. "What's to stop me from just going through with the deal with Ace and cutting you out?"

The knot in my stomach turned to lead. In that moment, I knew exactly who I was dealing with --- someone who'd smile while he stabbed you in the back.

The next day, I called Ace. I told them the truth; that I was no longer going to be working for Nevulis and be able to support the brands I had just sold them on. I expected them to thank me for the tip and hang up. Instead, they surprised me. They didn't care about Nevulis's brands. What they cared about was me --- they wanted me. My knowledge. My ability to walk into a bar and sell not just a keg but a story.

That's when they made the offer. A job. Straight up.

I walked into Nevulis thinking I was helping build someone else's future. Turns out I was building my own.

### Job #55 – In-Store Demos – Age 47 – 2011

After losing my salary at Nevulis, I had to find something that plugged the holes, even if it wasn't glamorous. Danielle, one of my co-workers, told me about a side hustle: demoing **Aidells** sausages in grocery stores. At first it sounded ridiculous --- a man who'd spent years selling everything from mortgages, to insurance, to craft beer and convincing bar managers to gamble on IPAs now reduced to handing out toothpicks in the meat aisle. But money is money, and I said yes.

Aidells made it idiot-proof. They handed me a kit like I was being deployed to some strange suburban battlefield: folding table, branded tablecloth, cooler, extension cord, electric skillet, tongs, toothpicks, even a giant branded umbrella so shoppers couldn't miss me between the frozen peas and DiGiorno's. The ace in the hole was the stack of coupons. Free packages of sausage, as many as I needed. Instead of hauling in product, I just raided the cooler case and charged it back with coupons. Zero cost, zero hassle.

The shifts were short --- three hours, in and out --- but the grind was the same as any sales job. Heat, pitch, repeat. Fire up the skillet until the aisle smelled like garlicky heaven, spear a sizzling sample, hand it over with a smile. The price point was higher than the competitors, but a bite of hot sausage on a toothpick erases hesitation fast. People who had never heard of Aidells were suddenly tossing three packs into their cart.

For me, it was almost comical. I'd spent years selling interest rates, life insurance and explaining IBUs and Belgian yeast strains to skeptical drinkers. Now I was slinging bite-sized pork to soccer moms and retirees in sweatpants, and the conversion rate was better. By the end of most demos, the shelves were empty, the cooler case stripped bare. Sometimes the store manager would walk by wide-eyed, wondering how the hell I had sold all the sausage in the sausage isle in just a few hours.

It wasn't glamorous. One day a week, three hours at a time, selling sausages like they were contraband. But it scratched the same itch as selling beer. The pitch, the performance, the satisfaction of seeing the product move. When I packed up, the skillet still hot and the umbrella folded under my arm, I felt the same weird pride I'd get after a good tap takeover.

On paper, it looked like a step down. From craft beer evangelist to sausage hawker. But to me, it was just another hustle, another absurd entry in a résumé already littered with side gigs and reinventions. And damned if I didn't enjoy it a little.

### Job #56 – Craft Beer Rep – Age 47 – 2011

**Ace Distributing** wasn't Nevulis. Nevulis had been a punchline with invoices. Warm kegs sweating in office closets, one delivery truck for eight sales reps, promises written on scrap paper that never turned into beer on the shelves. Ace, by contrast, was built on Miller and Coors.

Old-school. Reliable. You could've shut your eyes, rolled dice, and still hit an account pouring Miller Lite, Coors Light, or even an occasional High Life. The brands sold themselves --- neon signs glowing in every window, TV ads doing the heavy lifting. Being a domestic rep at Ace meant taking orders, hanging swag, making sure nobody ran out of light beer.

I wasn't brought in for that. They hired me to be the "craft beer guy," which in 2011 was still more of a curiosity than a career. My territory was South Central Pennsylvania, which meant walking into barrooms where Yuengling was oxygen. You didn't even order it by name. You asked for "a Lager," and a Yuengling appeared like gravity had pulled it from the tap. Miller outsold Bud in the region, a quirk that made Anheuser-Busch grind its teeth. Between Yuengling and Miller, the taps were sewn up so tight you couldn't pry one loose with a crowbar.

Trying to sell an IPA or an Imperial Stout in that landscape was like dragging a crate of avant-garde poetry into a tractor pull. Most of the time I got blank stares, sometimes open hostility. "What's wrong with Miller Lite?" --- "Nobody here drinks that hoppy shit" --- "Seven bucks a pint? Get the fuck out." Every call was a reminder that I wasn't in Philly, where craft was blooming, where beer bars and bottle shops were busy rewriting the rules. In York and Lancaster, I was a missionary carrying a gospel nobody wanted.

So I doubled down. Route during the day, tastings at night, tap takeovers on weekends, beer dinners whenever I could talk a restaurant into it. Beer dinners became my anchor. I leaned into my food background, pairing courses with styles --- wit beers with cheese plates, stouts with desserts, IPAs cutting through pork fat --- and tried to turn each night into a performance. I wanted people to leave not just fed, not just drunk, but convinced. Sometimes it worked. Enough small victories stacked up to keep me in the game. But the job was brutal. Six nights a week I was drinking "for work." I was basically a functioning alcoholic with a sales quota.

The irony was I never even applied to Ace. They came to me. They'd watched me grind at Nevulis and decided to poach me. No interview, no résumé. Just a handshake. They forgot one detail --- the drug test. Months later, HR realized, and I was frog-marched to a clinic with little warning.

I thought I could beat it. Quit smoking a few days before, drown myself in water, hope the test gods looked kindly. Wrong. I failed. Sitting in the office, I muttered something about "one hit at a party" like it was a parking ticket. By some miracle, they gave me a second chance. That night I stayed up until dawn reading internet forums filled with sketchy advice --- vinegar, detox teas, cranberry pills, gallons of water. The next morning I showed up with my bladder stretched like a balloon about to pop. I pissed clear and clean. Passed. Survival through desperation.

The bigger scare came later. I was out on the route when it hit --- stabbing pain that folded me over the steering wheel, sweat dripping, breath shallow. I limped into an urgent care where the doctor shrugged, ran a couple of half-assed tests, and told me to call my GI. It was Friday, after five. I went home and spent the weekend in pain, gambling with my insides.

Monday morning, my GI nearly fainted. The scans showed my diverticulitis had perforated. My colon had literally torn open, and the only reason I wasn't dead was that another section of intestine had sealed the hole like a cork in a bottle. She told me she'd never seen anything like it. Three weeks later, when the infection cooled, they cut me open and removed nearly half my colon. I spent three months out of work, stitched, scarred, shuffling around the house like a boxer who'd been beaten senseless but somehow stayed standing.

Still, I returned and got the work done. Nate, the Craft Brand Manager, and I were basically an insurgency inside a Miller/Coors machine. What was seen as a necessary evil in a changing landscape. But we were often reminded of who "kept the lights on" and paid the bills. Slowly, painfully, the craft portfolio grew. And so did the Craft Beer Division and with it the overhead, as we now had a half dozen or so sales reps.

Yards Brewing was one of the first real wins. We built their presence account by account until it had roots. Eventually, Yards wanted their own rep in the region. I interviewed, got the nod, and jumped ship.

Not long after, Ace gutted their sales team. Everyone had to reapply for the same jobs --- same workload, lower pay. A few old-timers stayed. Most were replaced by younger, cheaper labor. My timing was perfect.

Ace was the bridge. Ugly, bloody, nearly fatal, but a bridge all the same. It carried me from hustling in obscurity to representing one of the biggest independent breweries in the state. The price was almost half my colon. But the payoff was that I survived it long enough to keep walking forward.


### Job #57 – Brewery Representative – Age 49 – 2013


**Yards Brewing** was the big leagues compared to distribution. At Ace, I was the hired gun trying to wedge IPAs into bars where Miller Lite was practically a birthright. At Yards, I wasn't just selling beer --- I was carrying the flag for the brewery. Back then, being a brewery rep still meant something. Distributor reps were a dime a dozen, showing up weekly with order sheets and neon clocks. A brewery rep walking in the door was a rarity. People perked up. It felt like a visiting dignitary had dropped by with kegs instead of speeches. A few years later, brewery reps would multiply like fruit flies, and nobody would care, but in that moment, there was still some shine on the job.

Yards wanted me to push Philadelphia Pale Ale. Great beer, wrong territory. This wasn't Philly. South Central Pennsylvania was Yuengling country. You didn't order it by name. You said "Lager," and the bartender poured Yuengling without breaking stride. Add in a market split between Ravens fans, Steelers fans, and Eagles fans, and nobody was exactly waving Philly pride in the streets of York or Harrisburg. I pitched a different angle. Lead with Brawler, a dark mild ale that hit the same notes Lager drinkers were used to, but with a little more grit, a little more story. It worked. Accounts signed on. Sales ticked up. Yards started to trust me to follow my gut.

I went all in. Tattooed the Brawler logo on my forearm ---
a bare-knuckled boxer squaring off against the devil. It
wasn't branding. It was belief, inked into my skin. The
accounts noticed. Conviction is contagious. When you're
willing to bleed for a brand, people believe you.

But I wasn't just handing out samples and begging for tap
handles. I built my accounts like you build a kitchen
brigade. Staff trained, managers educated, everybody in
the loop. I wanted bartenders to talk about Brawler with
the same ease they talked about Lager.

That approach cracked doors nobody thought I could
open. The Hotel Hershey, the kind of place that only
reserved beer dinners and staff training for actual
brewers, let me in. I stood in that ornate dining room,
talking malt and yeast to staff in pressed uniforms,
realizing just how far I'd come from sweating in deli
kitchens and loading trucks.

The hustle never stopped. Days spent selling, nights
spent drinking for work. Tastings, tap takeovers, bottle
shop events. Beer dinners became theater. My food
background gave me an edge --- I knew how to pair
saisons with cheese or throw a stout against dessert ---
but what sold it was performance. I wanted people to
leave with stories, not just stomachs full of food. That's
why accounts stuck with me. I didn't just sell them beer. I
sold them on the idea of being part of something bigger
than the next pint.

And there were perks. Salary, bonuses, and an expense
card that gave me a daily allowance to keep accounts
"entertained." Lunches, dinners, beers --- repeat until

liver damage. It was essentially a corporate bar tab with my name on it. Six nights a week I was out drinking. I told myself it was part of the job, and in a way it was, but the line between work and addiction blurred quickly. A lot of reps I knew wound up with DUIs. Some crashed harder than that. Somehow I dodged it. I called it luck, but it was more likely sheer, stubborn survival.

For several years, Yards felt like the pinnacle. Swagger, story, and a boxer tattooed on my arm to prove it. I built relationships, carried the brand into places it hadn't gone, and got to feel like I was part of the craft beer wave as it broke across the country. But under all the bar tabs and long drives, I was unraveling. The drinking wasn't just work anymore. The travel wore me down. The pressure of keeping the hustle alive never let up.

Yards was one of the best chapters of my beer career. It felt like more than a paycheck --- it felt like being part of a cultural shift. But the cracks were already forming, and I wasn't ready to admit how deep they ran.

## Job #58 – Director of Sales & Marketing – Age 52 – 2016

**Spring House Brewing** looked shiny on the outside --- stainless steel tanks, polished floors, the kind of showpiece you'd expect on a brewery tour where everything smells like sanitizer and promise. But under the hood, it was a ghost ship. They were brewing maybe twice a week, tanks sitting idle like giant sculptures of wasted ambition. Matt, one of the owners, also the brewer, called me in. Director of Sales and Marketing. A title that sounded like authority, but what he was really offering was a mop and a sinking deck.

First order of business was credibility. Spring House had already been tossed out of a major distributor for mismanagement, which in this business is like being branded with a scarlet letter. Once you're "the mess," the story follows you everywhere. I did what they'd never bothered to do: built Annual Business Plans. Schedules, priorities, volumes, timelines --- the kind of paperwork wholesalers eat like steak. When I dropped calendars and projections on their desks, they were stunned. The joke brewery from Lancaster suddenly looked like it knew what the hell it was doing.

And for a minute, it worked. Orders rolled in. Tanks fired up every day. Production couldn't keep pace, and I had to start cutting distributor orders in half. For a brief stretch, I thought maybe I'd done it --- turned a laughingstock into something respectable.

Then the bombs went off.

First it was a call from a retailer. Cans exploding. Not a metaphor --- actual explosions. Beer seeping into drywall, seams blown, labels shredded. Customers sending photos of six-packs that detonated in kitchens and cars like they were pipe bombs. I went into stores that looked like crime scenes, mopping up with my words while wholesalers glared at me like I'd personally armed the grenades.

The brewery swore it was a one-time glitch. I did the rounds, smoothed the anger, rebuilt trust. And then it happened again. More exploding cans, more wreckages, more fury. This time there was no patch. I had to order a full recall. Humiliating. Our biggest distributor dropped us on the spot. They told us flat out: "Three months of shelf stability or you're done." It was a lifeline made of thread, and everyone in the room knew it.

The final insult came with bonuses. I'd doubled sales, dragged the brand out of the ditch, faced down angry retailers while the brewers shrugged. When payout time came, I was told I didn't qualify. My numbers didn't hit the mark because their beer was blowing up in cars and kitchens. Their failures had shredded my work, and now I was the one left empty-handed. No money, no thanks, no recognition. Just a shrug.

I walked away.

I was proud of the work, proud of the structure I'd forced into a brewery that thought chaos was a business plan. But disgust doesn't begin to cover what I felt watching the ownership shrug off their wreckage. Spring House didn't just blow up in the market --- it blew up in my hands, and I was the one left smelling like stale beer and betrayal.

**Job #59 – MD Sales Representative – Age 52 – 2016**

Leaving Spring House felt like pulling my hand out of a fire. I went back to **Yards Brewing**, but my old Central PA territory was already spoken for. They dangled a bigger footprint instead --- Maryland, Northern Virginia, South Jersey. The commute was punishing, two hours some days, two and a half on the worst of them --- each way. But this was Baltimore. My city. My scars in the pavement, my DNA in the bars. I didn't hesitate.

Sliding back into Yards was easy. I knew the beer, the pitch, the rhythm. It was like shrugging into a leather jacket I hadn't worn in years --- familiar, broken in, still carrying the smell of smoke and nights I half remembered. What made it different this time were the reunions. Henninger's, where Kenny and Jane held court with food that still made me want to weep. Holy Frijoles, across the street from where I once tried to run Thredhed, catching up with Geoff over beers and old war stories. Those nights weren't sales calls. They were hauntings. Baltimore hadn't moved an inch, but I had, and the dissonance was equal parts comforting and unnerving.

But the beer world had moved. The age of the brewery rep as rock star was over. A few years earlier, walking into a bar with a Yards shirt on meant you were carrying a flag, something bigger than a paycheck. Now? Just another rep in a crowded room. Rotating taps had become the rule, sixtels replacing half-barrels, because no one wanted to commit to a full keg of anything. The industry had shifted from passion to math. Discounts, giveaways, branded junk to keep your beer on the line. Grandmothers were ordering IPAs now, asking about dry-hopping like it was common language. What had once been outlaw had become wallpaper.

Still, Yards had weight. They weren't hustling from the margins anymore. Resources, marketing muscle, and recognition gave me leverage the smaller breweries couldn't dream of. I leaned on it. Adjusted. Played the new game. It wasn't as intoxicating as the golden days, but it was still satisfying when it worked.

The highlight was Maryland Deathfest --- Baltimore's annual convergence of noise, sweat, and black t-shirts. We brewed Death Fest Ale, an exclusive draft that made Yards the only craft brand in the lineup. The sales volume wasn't the story. The value was being part of the culture, standing in that crush of sound and beer where nothing mattered but the moment. For me, it was full circle --- Baltimore, beer, metal, all colliding in one weekend. I even threw myself into the pit again, one last reckless offering to the gods of noise. I came out bruised, soaked, exhilarated. And old enough to know it was the last time.

Then came the body's betrayal. Sharp pain in my side, something I chalked up to kidneys or maybe just a bad stretch of back pain. The scans said otherwise. Kidney stone first, then something worse hiding behind it. My mitral valve was wrecked, my heart limping along at 25 percent capacity. The doctors looked at me like I was a ghost already. Their words were blunt --- "You could go at any moment."

Two surgeries. First the stone, then the chest cracked open for valve repair. Recovery meant three months stitched up, moving slow, scarred, learning to breathe with the knowledge that I'd been walking around like a bomb waiting for its timer to hit zero.

And then, like always, I went back. Back behind the wheel, back into the bars, back into the grind of selling beer. The only difference was the scar on my chest, the reminder that death had already knocked once and would be back to try the handle again.

## Job #60 – PA Sales Representative – Age 54 – 2018

On paper it looked like a clever hustle. Two Baltimore outfits, one foot in each camp. **Charm City Meadworks** on one side, **Oliver Brewing** on the other. Mead and beer --- not competitors, so no conflict. One paycheck split down the middle, all handled from Pennsylvania, so I wasn't burning hours of my life on I-83 traffic. It felt like balance, like I'd finally gamed the system.

But the companies were different species.

Charm City looked polished, professional, almost surgical. They had branding dialed in tight, sleek cans with a story that fit neatly into the growing "drink local" narrative in Baltimore. They had swag, software, release calendars mapped out six months ahead, actual training programs. It was what a modern beverage company was supposed to look like --- sharp edges, discipline, no wasted motion.

Oliver? The opposite. Chaotic, sloppy, drowning in its own noise. No flag to rally around, no core brands, just a churn of one-offs with names that read like rejected band flyers. They were chasing novelty for novelty's sake. I'd walk into an account one week with a porter, come back the next week and it was gone, replaced by a peach sour nobody had asked for. There was no trust to build, no story to tell, just a moving target that made me look like an idiot every time I opened my mouth.

And both of them --- both --- were lashed to the same so-called distributor. Distributor in name only. In practice, it was a glorified retail shop playing dress-up as a wholesaler. No quarterly meetings, no business plans, no accountability. They treated the three-tier system like a suggestion. And me? I was left trying to convince bars and stores that this rickety arrangement was somehow legitimate. It wasn't. I wasn't selling beer; I was bailing water out of a sinking boat with my bare hands.

At first, curiosity moved mead. A few bars put it on draft, a few stores took cases, just to see what the hell it was. But mead doesn't move like beer. It lingers. It sips instead of pours. Once it sat on shelves too long, managers didn't want a second round. Bars hated tying up a line for something that trickled instead of flowed. So I went into desperation mode --- samples, tastings, coaxing bartenders to pour free drinks just to get customers used to the flavor. It worked sometimes, but more often I just watched skepticism harden into "no thanks."

Oliver was worse. No identity, no consistency, no faith. Every account felt like starting from zero, every month a new round of awkward introductions. I wasn't selling beer anymore --- I was apologizing for it.

And the bigger problem was the industry itself. Craft beer had eaten itself alive. What started as passion and rebellion had devolved into carnival tricks. Glitter beer. Cereal milk stouts. Gummy bear sours. Tap lists turned into rotating carousels of one-offs, training drinkers to abandon loyalty and chase novelty. Margins shrank. Competition ballooned. What once felt like a movement now looked like a clown show, a parody of itself.

Standing there with a box of mead samples in one hand and an unbranded Oliver tap handle in the other, I realized I wasn't just fighting a bad distributor or a sloppy brewery --- I was fighting the corpse of an industry.

That's when it hit me. Beer wasn't the center of the universe anymore. Liquor and wine were outselling it by miles. The margins were better. The hustle cleaner. You didn't have to beg someone to buy vodka --- it was already on their shopping list.

Beer had given me a decade of stories, scars, and friendships. It had carried me into rooms I never would have entered otherwise. But now it was burning me out, bleeding me dry, making me complicit in its own collapse.

I didn't walk away bitter. Just clear-eyed. It was time to leave the pint glass behind. Time to pour something stronger. Time for a new hustle.


**Job #61 – Liquor Sales Rep – Age 55 – 2019**

The jump from beer to spirits should have felt like culture shock, but it didn't. The terrain was the same --- the same cracked sidewalks, neon bar signs, and sticky floors I'd been trudging through for years. The only difference was what I was dragging through the door. Instead of pitching the latest IPA with a clever pun on the label, I was walking in with Faber Spirits --- vodka, gin, rum --- a brand under the **Theobald & Oppenheimer** umbrella.

Faber wasn't fancy, but it was built to move. Price-pointed low enough for managers to nod without thinking, clean enough for bartenders to actually use. You didn't need a five-minute lecture on hops or malt bills to sell it. One glance at the margins and they were in. What hooked me wasn't the bottles themselves, though --- it was the programs I could build around them. Cocktail menus, pairing dinners, seasonal kits. The same itch I scratched with beer dinners came roaring back, only this time with more tools, more angles. I wasn't just selling booze; I was helping bars reinvent their menus, which made me look less like a salesman and more like a partner. That's the hustle I loved.

The crown jewel was McCleary's Pub in Marietta. The same river town where I'd once run the New Day Café. Walking into that bar with my portfolio and walking out with a full cocktail menu built on my spirits --- magical. A literal full-circle moment, standing a few blocks from the ghosts of my old restaurant, watching bartenders sling drinks with recipes exclusive to my brand. For a minute, it felt like the universe was handing me a wink.

And the money came. For once, it wasn't scraps or broken promises. I was one of only two reps in the company to hit the top tier for program-building, and the bonus checks proved it. I was also selling bar supplies so we covered all the bases , selling cocktail kits, tossing coasters and swag around like candy. Faber wasn't just liquor; it came with a whole arsenal of add-ons --- the kind of infrastructure I never had in the beer world. For a stretch, everything clicked.

Then the world stopped.

Covid bulldozed through everything. Bars and restaurants shuttered. Even the state liquor stores --- the Pennsylvania Liquor Control Board's fortress of bureaucracy --- locked their doors. Overnight, my entire customer base evaporated. Accounts I'd nurtured for months, whole bar programs I'd built, gone. For a brief and ridiculous window, the state allowed distilleries to sling bottles out of trucks in parking lots. So there we were, masked up, standing in lines six feet apart, handing off glass bottles of vodka in strip-mall asphalt like it was Prohibition. The absurdity of it was almost funny, until you looked at your bank account. Salaries were gone. Everything was commission-only. My livelihood slid from "comfortable" to "nonexistent" in the time it took to wash your hands.

Then came the hand sanitizer pivot. Hospitals were begging. Shelves were stripped. Purell was the new currency. Faber switched gears overnight, cranking sanitizer instead of spirits. Glass bottles that once carried vodka now carried germ-killer. Pallets flew out the door faster than we could fill them. For a manic stretch, it felt like salvation. Firehouses, police stations, hospitals --- all calling, all desperate. I'd never seen demand like it.

But the company botched it. Priced it too low, gave away margin, undercut their own reps by building backdoor distribution channels that skipped us entirely. Worst of all, they clawed back commissions they'd already promised --- stealing from their own sales team in the middle of a pandemic. It wasn't just bad business. It was betrayal.

The collapse was fast and ugly. What should have been a lifeline turned into quicksand. By the time Theobald & Oppenheimer declared bankruptcy, the whole structure had eaten itself alive. I didn't even make it to the bitter end --- I was laid off, just another body tossed out as the ship went under.

For the first time in my life, I filed for unemployment. After decades of hustling --- sixty-plus jobs, a résumé that looked like a ransom note --- I'd finally been knocked flat by something I couldn't grind my way through. It was humbling, infuriating, clarifying. The hustle had always been mine to control, until suddenly it wasn't.

I'd been selling the dream of cocktails and spirits, but what I was left with was silence --- the kind of silence where you finally hear yourself breathing, and you realize it's the first time you've stopped in years.

**Interlude – Unemployment – Covid**

For the first time in my life, I filed for unemployment. Not a side hustle drying up, not a bar closing, not a bad bet gone wrong --- but the whole goddamn world grinding to a halt. Sixty-plus jobs behind me, restaurants I'd opened, kitchens I'd sweated in, beers and spirits I'd shoved across sticky bars, all of it suddenly irrelevant. I wasn't fired. I wasn't laid off. I was just...unplugged. Standing still. A government check in the mail instead of cash in the till.

Days stopped having names. I smoked weed like it was medicine, though the only thing it treated was the yawning hole of time. Hours blurred into afternoons that bled into nights where I barely bothered with dinner. The TV was wallpaper. The bong was the clock. I wasn't depressed exactly --- more sedated, embalmed, like I was watching myself dissolve into the couch.

Out of that fog came noise. I downloaded some recording software, dug an old mic out of a closet, and started messing around. No guitars, no sweat-soaked amps in basements, no bandmates bitching about chord changes. Just me and a laptop. What came out didn't sound like me at all --- part EDM, part dance, part alien transmissions from a guy I didn't recognize. I called it Pro Deuce and dumped it online, a breadcrumb trail of a stoned man trying to stay busy while the world collapsed. It's still floating around on Spotify today, a ghost of that strange chapter, something born out of boredom and smoke.

But weed has a way of holding you in place. Eventually even I got sick of myself --- sick of the haze, sick of the drift, sick of living inside a fogged fishbowl. Somewhere in there, I enrolled in truck driving school. It felt absurd at first, like a punchline. From craft beer dinners to CDL manuals, from cocktail menus to air brake systems. I switched gears --- literally.

The hardest part wasn't grinding through parallel parking a rig the size of a house. It wasn't keeping logbooks or sweating through a driving test with an instructor glaring from the passenger seat. The real terror was letting go of weed. A CDL meant random drug tests. Weed doesn't vanish in a day --- it lingers, clings to your blood like a bad habit that refuses to leave. So I quit. For the first time since I was a kid, I put it down completely.

I just passed my five-year anniversary clean. Even now, saying that feels like I'm lying to myself. Five years without the crutch that had carried me through every dive bar, every sleepless night, every busted job. But that's what it took to trade haze for asphalt, a buzz for a paycheck.

Unemployment didn't feel like a pivot at the time. It felt like rot, like idling in neutral while the world raced past. Only later did I see what it had done. It stripped me down, cut out the excuses, forced me to throw myself at something new. I went in burned out, stoned, restless. I came out with a license, a scar where the crutch used to be, and a new kind of road under my wheels.

**Job #62 – Truck Driver – Age 57 – 2021**

Truck driving school barely got me across the finish line. The CDL test was a blur of grinding gears and white-knuckled backing attempts, and when I walked away with a license in hand it felt less like triumph than a clerical error. I knew just enough to be dangerous. Still, the world needed truckers and **Schneider** was hiring. They had training, a sign-on bonus, and a reputation for at least pretending to give a shit. That was good enough.

Training was fast and merciless. Two weeks of classroom theory and roadwork, one week over the road, crammed into a cab with a trainer who grunted instructions, and then suddenly the keys were in my hand. No buffer. No easing into it. Just me behind the wheel of a machine longer than a house and heavier than sin, expected to roll solo.

My first assignment was regional --- five and a half days out, a day and a half home if I was lucky. Mondays started early and Saturdays ended late. It wasn't glamorous. It wasn't even tolerable. But it was the foot wedged in the door of a new trade, and I couldn't afford to slam it shut.

The schedule chewed me up, but the real terror wasn't the grind. It was backing. Every rookie knows it. You can drive 500 miles without blinking, but if you can't snake a 53-footer into a dock without turning it into modern art, you're dead weight. Truck stops were off-limits for me at first --- too many eyes, too many angles, too much chance of making an ass of myself. I hid in highway pull-offs, rest areas, and parking lots with wide-open exits. It was cowardly, but it kept the panic at bay.

Rest areas had their own cost. Some had no bathrooms. Others had porta-potties that smelled like the aftermath of a county fair in August. That's when I learned the truth about the plastic bottles littering highway shoulders. They weren't trash. They were testimony. Nobody lines up bottles of piss because they want to. It's survival.

My real baptism came on my first solo run. Dispatch wanted to ease me in with a short hop, a run that should've had me home before dinner. All I had to do was scale the load at a Pilot truck stop. Simple. Unless, like me, you miss the truck entrance and roll into the car lot instead.

One wrong turn and I was trapped in a restaurant parking lot designed for sedans, not semi-trailers. I was boxed in by curbs, compact cars, pedestrians, and the mounting weight of my own failure. My trailer blocked half the lot. My hands locked on the wheel. Sweat rolled down my back in sheets. I muttered every curse I knew, convinced I'd made the worst mistake of my life.

Then she appeared --- another trucker, older, sharp-eyed, carrying herself like someone who had already seen every rookie meltdown twice over. She parked her rig, walked straight into the chaos, and started flagging me like a runway marshal. Arms waving, shouting directions, blocking traffic, shooing pedestrians out of harm's way. For 45 minutes I lurched back and forth, stalling, grinding, inching my way out of that asphalt mousetrap under her watchful command.

When I finally cleared the lot, I wanted to disappear, park the truck, hand in the keys, and never be seen again.

Instead I climbed down, shaking, and thanked her like she had just pulled me out of a burning building. She shrugged. For her, it was Tuesday. For me, it was the first time I understood how merciless this world was --- and how saving grace sometimes came from the driver in the next cab.

That was trucking. Brutal, humiliating, humbling. It broke you down in ways you didn't expect. But every day I rolled another mile, corrected another mistake, learned to live with the grind. Slowly, painfully, I started to believe that maybe I did belong out there after all.

### Job #63 – Truck Driver – Age 57 – 2021

Four months into Schneider and I already knew I was meat in the grinder. Then the phone rang. **JB Hunt**. Same recruiter who had brushed me off after trucking school now suddenly had a different tone. Back then I was green, a liability, a man with a license but no proof.

Now, three months of white-knuckle solo runs had magically transformed me into an "experienced driver." Translation: I could make them money.

I wasn't sentimental about it. I wasn't out here chasing sunsets or "the freedom of the open road." I was chasing paychecks. So I jumped.

The first assignment had me running groceries for Giant Food out of a terminal that split its runs between dry van and reefers. Second shift. Three to six in the evening start times, twelve to fourteen-hour days, five days a week. Slip seating was the rule. You never had your own truck. You borrowed whatever steel box had just rolled in from the shift before. Sometimes it smelled like a Febreze commercial. More often it reeked of spilled coffee, grease, and a driver's bad hygiene. You climbed into someone else's filth and made it yours for twelve hours. Then you handed it back like a dirty rental car.

Every new store was its own puzzle. The first run was always a nightmare. You never knew what kind of dock you were walking into. Blind corners that forced you to back in without ever seeing the hole. Angled slots so tight you had to bend the trailer like a paperclip. Alleys where pedestrians strolled past like you weren't dragging 80,000 pounds of groceries behind you. Once you figured it out, you could breathe. But that first time? It was like threading a needle with shaking hands and a live audience.

And this wasn't a no-touch job. This was driver-assist. That meant pulling pallets off with an electric jack and rolling them through the bowels of fluorescent-lit grocery store back rooms. When the pallets were wrapped tight and clean, it was tolerable. When the shipper cut corners, it was hell. Loads shifted. Pallets collapsed. Suddenly you were ankle-deep in grape jelly, scooping glass and purple sludge off the trailer floor, re-palleting the mess while the clock ticked unpaid. Flour bags went off like powder bombs. Yogurt cartons bled across the deck. Cans scattered like marbles on asphalt. Every door you opened was a coin toss --- clean delivery or slow-motion disaster.

The money? Not what they promised. Recruiters are paid to lie. I should've known better. When I pressed management, they tossed me a lifeline: intermodal. "That's where the money is," they said. "You're dependable. We don't want to lose you."

So I transferred. New terminal. New promises. New flavor of misery.

Intermodal wasn't trucking in the romantic sense. It was scavenger hunting. Rail yards that stretched for miles, containers stacked like Lego bricks by someone who hated symmetry. Half your shift was spent hunting down the right box. The other half was spent sitting at crossings, trapped while endless freight trains clattered by, graffiti-tagged steel rolling past for thirty minutes at a stretch. All unpaid. Time evaporating. Sanity fraying.

It wasn't skill anymore. It was endurance. Patience. Willingness to eat hours of your life without pay and call it a job.

I stuck it out for a year. A solid year of late nights, broken pallets, and rail yard purgatory. By the end I knew what I had known from the start --- the recruiter's pitch was smoke, mirrors, and bullshit. The money wasn't there. The promises dissolved like sugar in hot coffee. Same story I'd seen in restaurants, beer, liquor. Different uniform, same scam. They sell you the dream, then hand you the mop.

So I started looking again.

## Job #64 – Truck Driver – Age 58 – 2022

**Quality Carriers**. The name sounded like something you'd see on a box of discount cereal, not painted on the side of a truck hauling powdered chemicals. Their bread and butter was dry bulk pneumatic tankers --- long silver cigars on wheels that looked like props from a Cold War sci-fi flick. They were designed to haul anything fine enough to be blown through a hose: flour, cement powder, coal flakes, even little stones ground to dust. Loading was simple: dump it in from the top, seal the hatch, then use air pressure and hoses to shoot it into silos or holding tanks on the other end. Imagine plumbing with explosives. That was pneumatic tanker life.

I didn't touch much of it. They had a dry van division that was short on drivers, and since the pay was the same, I went that route. Dry van might not have had the "wow factor" of a metal lung full of powdered limestone, but it was cleaner, less fiddly, and familiar. I didn't need a crash course in physics every time I hooked up a trailer.

This was a regional gig --- mostly Carolina runs, two or three overnights a week. Dispatch kept me moving Monday through Friday, with the occasional Saturday thrown in for good measure. Compared to the endless, bone-grinding coast-to-coast hauls I'd seen other guys swallow whole, it felt almost civilized.

The road at night had its rhythm. Loneliness, yes, but also space to breathe. I set my truck up like a rolling apartment. A fridge wedged into one corner, a microwave strapped down with bungee cords, a battered coffee pot balanced on a shelf, a tablet rigged for streaming when I wanted company. I meal-planned like a survivalist. No midnight drive-thru disasters. No gut bombs disguised as cheeseburgers under heat lamps. Leftovers from my own fridge, reheated at midnight while parked on gravel. Fresh coffee from my own pot while the rest of the lot lined up at Subway. In a world of chaos and diesel fumes, my sleeper felt like a tiny square of order --- a capsule hotel barreling down I-81.

And the pay? For once, no lies. No recruiter's magician act. No waiting for the "real" money to show up after a probationary period. The checks matched the pitch. After years of smoke and mirrors, it almost felt suspicious. A straight deal in trucking --- rare enough to taste like luxury.

But there's always a catch, and in this line of work, it's spelled P-A-R-K-I-N-G. On the East Coast, parking is a blood sport. If you're not shut down by four in the afternoon, you're screwed. By the time I rolled south and hit the Carolinas around midnight, every space in every truck stop was gone. Paid reservations were supposed to guarantee a slot, but more than once I rolled in, bone-tired after fourteen hours, only to find some other driver already wedged into my spot. At two in the morning, arguments over painted asphalt are about as civilized as prison yard disputes. Sometimes it ended in shouting. Sometimes in threats of fists. Most nights you just drove on, praying for a hole in the dark.

Still, the job wasn't bad. The miles stacked up, the checks cleared, and my rolling apartment kept me sane. But after a while, the overnights wore me down. No microwave meal or Netflix stream can replace sleeping in your own bed, under your own roof, with silence that doesn't hum like diesel. Eventually the balance tipped. Money or home? For once, I wanted home.

So I started looking again.

**Job #65 – Truck Driver – Age 60 – 2024**

**S&H Express** ran out of York. For me, that meant twenty fewer minutes each way. Forty minutes shaved off a round trip doesn't look like much on paper, but behind the wheel it feels like someone just handed you a gift card for time itself. Truckers measure life in miles, minutes, and exits --- cut enough of them and you start to feel like you're stealing back something that had been owed all along.

This was home-daily work, which meant no more half-weeks on the road, no more watching my beard grow in a side mirror parked at some overcrowded rest stop. I left at six in the morning, rolled back into York anywhere between six and eight at night. Twelve, fourteen-hour days, but the difference was staggering. When I killed the engine at night, I wasn't listening to another diesel hum through the paper-thin walls of a sleeper. I was stepping into my own house, my own bed, my own silence. After a year of living by truck stop schedules, that felt like oxygen.

But trucking doesn't let you have wins without taxing them. The hours still stacked up like poker chips, and at sixty I started thinking less about miles and more about mortality. You sit in that cab long enough and you feel your spine compressing, your blood thickening. I'd read somewhere that truckers lived shorter lives than most workers --- didn't need the statistic to believe it. The road has a way of grinding you down slowly, feeding you fast food and stress until the only thing left in the tank is resentment.

Most of my runs were to New Jersey. If Dante had written a trucking edition of Inferno, Jersey would be a circle all its own. Jug handles that fling you into traffic like a carnival ride, buttonhook turns designed for wagons and horses, not fifty-three-foot trailers, and docks hidden like afterthoughts behind chain link and potholes. The traffic alone could break a monk --- a demolition derby of box trucks, sedans, and pissed-off commuters who all drove like they had an appointment with the devil. By the time I crossed back into Pennsylvania, I felt like I'd survived a street fight I hadn't signed up for.

Every day chipped away at me in increments --- a dock with six inches of clearance, a four-wheeler cutting across my nose on the Turnpike, another warehouse manager barking orders like I'd volunteered for military service. And yet, when I rolled back into my lot, parked the truck, and pointed my car toward home, the worst of it fell off me. The one payoff --- the only one that mattered --- was pulling into my own driveway, shutting the door behind me, and knowing I'd be sleeping in my own bed.

S&H kept their word, and in trucking that's worth something. The checks matched the promises; the work was steady. But the Jersey grind gnawed at me, and eventually the familiar itch came back --- the same one that had carried me through sixty-odd jobs already. Somewhere out there was another offer, another hustle, another promise of just a little more. And like a moth circling a flame, I felt myself leaning toward it, even as the smell of diesel still clung to my clothes.

### Job #66 – Truck Driver – Age 61 – 2025

My wife has this reflex. The second I start grumbling about work, a help wanted ad lands in my inbox. She's not wrong to do it. It's her way of saying, then go do something else instead of bitching about it. One morning she sent me one that looked like the holy grail --- local runs, home every night, nine or ten hours behind the wheel instead of twelve to fourteen. The pay looked solid too. For a minute, I thought maybe I'd stumbled on the kind of gig truckers whisper about but never actually see.

The fine print? It was a fuel tanker job. Gasoline, diesel, hazmat placards plastered on the sides, the whole deal. The kind of load that could turn you and half a Wawa into a news story if you sneezed wrong. I called Dave, an owner-operator with a small fleet who contracted through **Penn Tank Lines**. He laid it out like a salesman who's already counting your money. "Nine or ten hours a day. Good pay. Twelve on paper because it's a slip seat." Slip seat means the truck never sleeps --- you finish your shift, someone else takes the same rig out. No comfort in ownership, just a constant relay. But I bit. After a labyrinth of applications and background checks, I was hired.

Six months later, the shine's gone. The hours are long, the money's short, and the promise looks like another bait-and-switch I should've seen coming. Some days there's no work at all. Nothing like climbing into a tanker with hazmat paperwork, driving all day, risking everything, and ending up with less than you were told. At sixty-one, I should've learned, but apparently I'm still the guy who believes the pitch. Another layer of wool over the eyes, another hustle exposed.

But something's different this time. The job is just a job. There's something else simmering in the background, something bigger. I've started a nonprofit --- the **Workforce Education Fund** --- built to raise money for people who need vocational training, who can't afford tuition or tools. It's not a dream anymore; it's paperwork filed, board assembled, EIN issued, and 501(c)(3) status with the IRS. Check us out at: www.WorkforceEducationFund.com

It feels like the closest thing to permanence I've ever put my hands on.

And maybe that's the point. By the time this book makes it into your hands, I might have another job to tack on. Maybe #67, #68, who knows. That's been the rhythm all along. But for once, I get to claim two titles that don't depend on anyone's promises, anyone's payroll, anyone's bait-and-switch.

Author. Publisher.

Those ones stick.

## Final Thoughts

Sixty-six jobs, give or take. That's not a résumé; it's a crime scene. Every one left something behind --- a scar, a debt, a half-decent meal, or a story I couldn't shake. Kitchens, bars, trucks, basements, boardrooms --- they bleed together if you squint, a long smear of grease, sweat, and fluorescent lighting. Some gigs fed me. Some broke me. Some chewed me up and left me coughing out the pieces in parking lots at two in the morning. And yet here I am --- still standing, still hustling, still looking for the next hustle even when I swear I'm done.

If you came here looking for a moral, some neat Hallmark wisdom, you're in the wrong book. There isn't one. This isn't a roadmap or a career guide. It's more like a field manual you find at the bottom of a duffel bag --- pages ripped, stains on the corners, scribbled notes about how not to get fired, how to bluff your way through the night, how to keep your head down until the check clears. Work never defined me, but it sure as hell shaped me. Every shift was a lesson, every layoff a reminder, every bad boss another scar layer hammered onto the hide.

I used to envy the lifers --- the ones who picked a lane, stayed there, collected promotions and pensions, and left the building with a cake and a gold watch. But I've seen those people too. I've seen what routine does when it hardens into a coffin you climb into willingly. Comfort kills, just slower than cocaine. I didn't want to be embalmed in routine. I wanted the scenic route, the crooked path through every dive bar, kitchen, truck stop, and boardroom that would let me in the door.

What I learned is this --- there's dignity in grease burns, clarity in bone-deep exhaustion, and a kind of comedy in the middle of disaster if you're twisted enough to look for it. The hours you spend mopping up grape jelly or watching a colon surgeon peel half your guts out aren't wasted if you walk away with the story.

This book is proof that a crooked résumé still adds up to a life. Call me Jack of all trades, master of none if you want --- I'll take it. I call it survivor of many, builder of stories, collector of scars.

And now, somehow, I'm an author. A publisher. Titles I never chased, never expected, but here they are, stamped onto me like the others. By the time you read this, maybe I'll be on job number sixty-seven, or sixty-eight. Maybe I'll still be climbing into a truck before dawn, maybe I'll be selling another dream, maybe I'll be sitting at a desk trying to wrangle a whole different hustle. Doesn't matter.

The work doesn't end until you do. Until then --- you keep moving, keep hustling, keep writing the story one shift at a time.

## Acknowledgments

A special thanks to Hilary, Jahna and Simon for giving me a reason. And to Mom, Dad (RIP), Mary, Joe and the rest of my family for supporting me through it all.

## About the Author

Peter Belz is a writer, musician, cook, photographer, truck driver --- well, I could spend all day listing all the things he's done --- suffice to say, Jack of all Trades. He is currently living in Lancaster, PA. This is his debut memoir, published by J&S Press.

A little bird

Flew in a tree

Upon a limb

To sit

When I looked up

To see the bird

I didn't know those damn things

Spit